Mission

John Alite and S.C. Pike have a common goal, a message to the
world, one they wanted to convey within the Darkest Hour Series.
They hope to inspire those of all ages, who are struggling in life, to
persevere, and to never give up or give in to a
life of crime, no matter the circumstances one finds themselves in.

There is always Hope, Faith, and God.

JOHN ALITE
DARKEST HOUR

BY

S C P I K E

A True Story

Book One of Series: S.C. Pike has written John Alite'
biography, starting with his childhood, going into his
teenage years, and then into adulthood. All the
transformations and events within his life have been
documented with precision, and are true accounts of h
John Alite found himself involved with organized Crin
Mainly with the New York Mafia, (also known as Cos
Nostra), Gang members, and mob affiliates. Drugs an
Violence.

DARKEST HOUR
A True Story / True Crime
~~*

S.C. Pike brings John Alite's story to life in such a
it will make the reader feel they are living in his sh
Starting from a young age and moving into adulthood,
reader will come to have an appreciation for all
influences that swayed Mr. Alite to succumb to living a
of crime.

Former Mafia Enforcer for John Gotti and the Gamb
Crime Family, John Alite, shares his life story in a uni
way, in hopes to dispel the mystique of the mob and s
anyone from living a life of crime.

~~*

He's had too many darkest hours to count, but he's pushed through them all with a spirited perseverance, tenacity of mind, and a strength of purpose. Just like everything else in his life, he's met adversity head on with fierce determination and a resoluteness to come out on top.

~~*

A college baseball scholarship was his way out of the inner city, but his dreams of going pro were crushed by an arm injury.

John Alite was forced to return home to the only life he knew, where having to live on the streets of New York meant one thing—learning how to survive.

He was driven.
He was extreme.
He was feared.
But most of all, he was loyal.

From a young age, he found himself influenced by the wrong crowd. Enticed by the wealth, power, and prestige of the mafia, he immersed himself in a world that was foreign to most. A society where policies were enforced by instilling fear.

Those at the top were about obtaining and harnessing absolute power, while covertly using their own warped codes of ethics. Honor and loyalty were merely a misnomer. The cold, bitter truth was, he was expendal and his sworn allegiance was rewarded with betrayal.

On the run and unable to trust anyone, John was fin: forced to confront his own demon—himself. Facing harsh realities of who he was and what he had done wa? pretty, and he had some serious, life-altering decisions make. Ones that would come with a price.

Through a life of heartache, betrayal, and loss come story of grace, healing, and redemption.

~~*

John Alite has made it his life's mission to dispel mystique of the mafia and sway anyone from living a of crime. His goal is to inspire and help as many troub kids as possible.

~~*

Author S.C. Pike is one of the first women to step into mafia genre and write about the true story, intimate and experiences of Former Mafia Enforcer John A from a first person point of view. She brings his story life in such a way it will make the reader feel they are liv in his shoes. Starting from a young age and moving in adulthood, the reader will come to have an appreciat for all the influences that swayed Mr. Alite to succumb living a life of crime.

Preface

I am convinced everything happens for a reason, and there's a purpose why I'm alive today to tell my story. I have been given a second chance at life, and I'd like to believe God chose to use me to reach troubled kids. This has become my new passion, my newfound adrenaline rush. I feel called to educate and help prevent the younger generation from following in my footsteps. This new mindset of mine, this second chance I have at life, I want to spend it living a life worthy of God.

I'm of the opinion God can take our poor decisions, its circumstances, and all the aftermath from our crumbled pasts and turn them around, using our experiences to his glory. My hope, my motivation, is if I can influence just one kid in such a way as to keep them from going down the wrong path, then I will have served a greater purpose in life.

2 Corinthians 10:7

You are judging by appearances.
If anyone is confident that they
belong to Christ, they should
consider again that we belong to Christ
just as much as they do.

Chapter 1

Whether my dad likes to acknowledge it or not, he trained me to be a killer. Obviously, those weren't his intentions when he raised me to be a fearless fighter, but somewhere along the way those goals became mine. I'm not blaming my father for the way he raised me, nor am I making excuses for having been raised within a turbulent home life as well as being immersed in a very violent and hostile era.

The choices I've made in the past are mine, and I take full responsibility for them. I always have. I had made one poor decision after another, allowing myself to descend down a very dark road filled with unlawful, fraudulent, and villainous deeds. Only one person was responsible for my path, and that was me.

I was convinced I'd be invincible against the pitfalls, and exempt from the betrayal of those closest to me. In all actuality, the underworld was nothing but one big quagmire of deception, double-dealings, and double-crossings. The mob life was unpredictable at best, and sooner or later, the treacherous lifestyle would inevitably catch up to me. It was a painful pill to swallow when I realized I wasn't as bulletproof as I'd originally thought. I was wrong on so many levels, and it cost me.

It was never my objective to be an enforcer for the mafia. It wasn't like I had spent my childhood dreaming of one day becoming a famous criminal, or worse, a killer. I'd tried everything possible to keep from turning to the streets in order to make a living. As a child, the minute I could swing a bat or throw a punch, I dreamt of becoming a professional baseball player or a boxer. I wanted to be the best at everything and anything I set my mind to, so I became obsessed with aspirations of going pro.

As early as I could walk, my father poured his heart and soul into training my older brother and me to be extremely proactive, highly aggressive, and savagely fearless. Just as one would train for the Olympics from a young age, we were forced into a daily regiment of workouts. I was doing pushups and pull-ups like a new military recruit by the age of four. The physical training we were subjected to was punishing, grueling, and most likely considered inhumane among today's society, but I loved it. It's hard for most to imagine that I was forced into fighting and boxing on a daily basis all before first grade. Mandated actually, but it was all I knew. From the beginning, I not only thrived in this type of an environment, but I also soaked up every one of my father's ideologies and doctrines.

A hard, resounding slap to the side of my face, pulls me from my thoughts, leaving a prickly, stinging sensation in its wake. I don't even flinch. I blink a couple of times then focus my attention on my father who's standing before me.

"Are you listening to me!" my dad shouts in Albanian. He always spoke, or yelled, in his native tongue at home depending on his mood.

"I hear ya," I tell him as he whacks me on the side of the head again for good measure. Even at nineteen he still hits me, but I've never once thought about hitting him back, or sizing him up. I love him unconditionally so I never felt the need to challenge him; I still don't. He's my hero.

I was brought up in a highly aggressive family in all aspects of life. The physical abuse I'd encountered in my formative years would've had Child Protective Services beating down our door.

My mother suffered the same fate as her children. Being Albanian, she didn't have a say. This was simply part of our culture. All the women in our household were molded the old-fashioned way: their job was to cook and clean while the men always came first.

I was surrounded by hostility and violent behavior. It was doled out mainly by my father, but my brother and uncles did so as well without giving it a second thought. Heck, even our neighbor, who was a good friend of my father's, was allowed to hit us. My brother, two sisters, and I didn't know any different. There was no reason to question the abuse, because it was our norm. Being hit my entire life was simply the world I lived in. Then obviously there's the streets which were far more ruthless and unforgiving no matter what age.

The fear of getting hit was never a problem for me. I suppose that was because I didn't have a choice but to confront danger head on, and quickly adapt, knowing I wasn't allowed to back down. Whether I wanted to or not, I was also forced into fights. My father would bring other kids over to the house and make us fight them, to "toughen us up." I was taught how not to care if I got hurt, or worse, when I got a broken nose or bone. There was no quitting for me, the fight had to go on until someone couldn't get up. Blocking out pain became an artform. That combined with the lack of fear I'd acquired over the years were the main reasons why I caught so many beatings at home and on the street.

Everyone in our house communicated by yelling and screaming. The physical fighting every bit equal to the verbal assaults, and it didn't take long before I became immune to it all. I guess because of this I grew numb to empathy and compassion, having lost the ability to understand and share other's feelings and pains, but I still tried to be fair to people. Although, the lines sometimes blurred between discerning whether or not to grant someone on the wrong side of my path any leniency or not.

Granting mercy wasn't something my world was capable of grasping. It was survival of the boldest, and the most fearless, and the ones who survived on the streets where the ones who were most feared. I learned that lesson as early as elementary school. I *had* to become indifferent to the violence that surrounded me within the public schools and on the streets.

"You need to go back to boxing," my dad informs me callously, hell-bent on solving this problem of mine overnight.

"Yeah, sure," I say, backing up a step to avoid his fists again. I had been granted a full baseball scholarship from the University of Tampa. I played varsity baseball all four years in high school; the last two as team captain. My achievements were surreal, and the hard work had paid off, but only two months in I injured my throwing arm. This wasn't the first time I had compromised my arm, but this time, there was unrepairable damage.

It was my junior year in high school when it all caught up to me, and I ignored it. I'd been playing on three to four teams at the same time in any given season to keep my skill level high, and I overthrew. The doctor I had seen was actually in charge of the New York Mets and he knew immediately what my injury was. He recommended surgery, but my college coach disagreed.

My coach wanted me to try cortisone shots instead, which I did. Looking back, it was probably the wrong thing to do, because I didn't let up on my training.

Abusing my arm this way, it was inevitable it would give out on me. I just didn't think it'd cripple my ability to play baseball.

By the end of my first semester of college the pain had become so excruciating, I wound up going through Tommy John's Surgery. The healing phase was the worst, simply because I wanted immediate results. Instead, I endured weeks of physical therapy and with each passing week, it became more than clear my arm was not going to perform for me the way it once did. My career as a baseball player was over.

With my entire future up in smoke, the discouragement and disappointment consumed me; the emotions mixed together in my chest like a two-part epoxy glue, quickly thickening, constricting my breathing. I've just had my fucking soul ripped out, and my father didn't give me time to digest the turn of events.

"I'll go to the gym tomorrow and talk to Vic, start making plans for boxing," I tell him.

"Good." He nods, satisfied. Happy I was going to get back on my feet and not wallow in self-pity.

"I'll give boxing another shot even though I have my doubts."

With a fierce look in my father's eyes, he steps forward and jams his finger into my chest. "You *will* beat this," he demanded. I almost smile at his obstinate pursuit of never allowing a few road blocks to stand in the way of reaching a goal."

I take a deep breath, and suck it up, agreeing, "I'll beat it, dad." The sparkle in my eye tells him I will give it my all. He's the one who trained me to be obsessively driven after-all. I live to impress him, but above all, I love to show him just how strong-minded and spirited he raised me to be.

He stands before me, looking proud of his protégé, and I take a moment to bask in his silent approval. With a look of pride in his eyes, he gives me a quick jerk of his chin, his way of telling me how proud he is of me despite the turn of events. With the conversation over, he turns around and leaves my bedroom.

I let out a huge breath as I think about how screwed up my life has just become. The thing about planning your future around sports—today you have a career, then tomorrow you don't. My dad never put stock into book smarts, therefore, school was never impressed upon us as being important.

The silence in my bedroom overtakes me. Just this morning I had to de-register from the University of Tampa, informing my coach of the bad news. I sit down on the edge of my bed, letting out a frustrated growl and run my fingers through my hair.

"You'll catch your break, I know you will," my brother says from his bed on the other side of the room, trying to console me. I pause, looking at him with skepticism.

Although we're only eleven months apart, my brother, Jimmy was the one with all the natural talent.

When it came to school and sports he excelled with very little effort whereas I had to work myself to the bone, sacrificing everything and anything in order to achieve my goals.

"I don't think you understand," I tell him with conviction, "baseball was more than just about catching a break, or being part of my life, it's who I am." My brother could've had any sports scholarship he wanted if he only applied himself, but he rode that wave of doing just enough to get by. I didn't just want to get by, I wanted to be king of the mountain.

Jimmy is laid out on his bed with his hands resting behind his head. He shifts his gaze to mine and replies in a solemn voice, "Oh, I understand disappointment, and I also know what it's like to lose."

I catch the look in his eyes before he turns away to stare up at the ceiling, his voice all-knowing. I take pause and study him, something I haven't done in a long time. Somewhere along the way we've grown apart. We used to be damn near inseparable. I'd always looked up to him with admiration, because things seemed to come so easy for him. With that statement, I guess things weren't as easy for him as they appeared.

I think all he'd ever wanted in life was to have our dad's approval, but he could never seem to acquire it. He wasn't a soldier of servitude like me, a puppy willing to please his master at the drop of a hat. I believe my brother despised our father's stringent standards, and as long as he resisted them, he was never going to gain his favor. It's just the way our father had always operated, and one just had to accept this about him, understanding that he was only doing the best he could for his boys, wanting better for us.

I wound up becoming a chip off the old block from the very beginning, but then took things a step further by becoming extreme in everything I did. Before I knew it, I had morphed into this aggressive and fiercely competitive young man. It all started out innocent enough, me wanting to make my father proud at any cost, but when the desire to supersede everything in all aspects of my life, I became something totally different, something that would prove to be very dangerous and feared among the streets.

~~*

The dynamics of what was taking place on the streets in New York in the mid-seventies to early-eighties was nothing short of pandemonium. This era was considered to be one of the most turbulent times in New York's history, and I was smack dab in the middle of it as a teenager.

The air was thick with tension. Everyone could feel the threat of a ticking time bomb looming overhead. The city was slowly imploding in on itself. It was like a scene from a movie, watching everything unfold, promising a cataclysmic event, and nothing could seem to stop it.

The Big Apple was dealing with more gang related violence and homicides in 1980 than ever before in history. Drug dealers were a dime a dozen with crack and heroin taking a front seat on the market. Both the dealers and gangs infested the city like a plague, taking the crime rate to new levels never seen before. At the same time, the prostitutes worked openly in mass numbers, available on every street corner. It didn't take long for New York to descend into utter chaos.

The black and Latino population had increased hand over fist within the city as well. Not just as a direct result from the end of the Vietnam war, but the government was busing in the minorities and the younger generation to attend school. Many of the wealthy and middle-class families fled for the suburban life in which the media called the White Flight. Those that stayed behind reacted violently to the ethnic changes. Racial tensions soared to an all-time high.

As if that wasn't enough to contend with, New York was experiencing an industrial decline and an economic stagnation which led to a dramatic downturn for America's largest city. With opportunities scarce, finding a decent job was almost impossible. The government had no spare funds to help aid our disabled veterans from the war. Without low-income housing assistance, many disabled soldiers found themselves homeless, living on the streets. These veterans suffered both mentally and physically, and in order for them to cope, they turned to substance abuse which further aided the drug market.

Growing up I was forced to confront violence and deal with things that most kids nowadays don't have to. My elementary, junior high, and high school years were not immune to the mayhem either. By the time I reached ninth grade, my entire high school was at each other's throats, and not just somebody here and there... it was everybody.

Armed police guards were stationed at all school exits, having locked us in with chains on the doors to keep other kids from trying to break in with the intent of hurting other kids. No one had even thought about the potential fire hazards this created. Worse than that, we were trapped inside having to contend with incorrigible kids selling drugs, and bullies doling out violence with a vengeance just because they could. It was insanity. Between the race wars and illicit drugs permeating every hallway at Franklin K. Lane High School it's a wonder we survived.

Unless one had lived through this era of pure hell of street combat, it would be impossible for them to comprehend the mass amounts of bloodshed and violence that had taken place in broad daylight and in front of children of all ages.

One would think book smarts would've been a great way to escape the nightmare I was living in, but no one really cared whether I excelled or failed academically. My education wasn't impressed upon me as being important. As long as I was in the basement of our house, training for pro-boxing or the major leagues, my father didn't care if I was at school or not. Academia was never part of our family atmosphere. What took precedence above all was athleticism.

Although it was a negative way to grow up, my father helped me to survive and thrive during one of the most dangerous and intense times known to the streets. I didn't mind taking on three guys at the same time even though I knew I'd be defeated. The concern for me wasn't getting physically hurt, it was the embarrassment of losing. That was my only concern in a brawl not to lose.

I became brutal... violent... and very dangerous. I was going to make sure the loser wasn't going to get back up for another shot at me again. My dad didn't care so much as to whether I won or lost a fight, his motto was just don't back down from anyone, because if you held your ground, they wouldn't come back.

It didn't matter if I was part of the violence or a witness to it, because it was instilled in me to be fearless, confronting danger head on with an aggression and a boldness in order to survive the streets. Having been exposed to such violence from a very young age, I suppose I had become desensitized to it all, because I never had to get over the shock factor of the brutalities which surrounded me on a daily basis.

~~*

This dream of my father's, however, came with a price. He just didn't know how driven or extreme I'd become in order to succeed at whatever it was I set my mind on.

Little did my father realize his fanatical methods of physical conditioning while instilling in me his belief system, he was actually training me to be something far different than an aggressive and fiercely competitive pro-boxer or baseball player.

All of this, every single situation I was thrust into growing up, my father had unknowingly trained me not only for the mob world, but as a killer too. The one thing I most understood by this point and time in my life... was violence.

Chapter 2

~ 10 YEARS EARLIER ~

All of us kids sit at the dinner table and exchange knowing glances. Each of us holding on to some small sliver of hope—maybe he won't notice. But I know that's just wishful thinking. All of us knew he was in a bad mood the second he walked up the stairs and into the kitchen. It wasn't the sound of his heavy shoes stomping with loud, menacing thuds with each step he took up the stairs to the second floor. It was much more obvious than that. It was because he was quiet. The pursed lips and the hard face only confirms it. The entire family knew when my father was overly quiet that it'd only be a matter of time before he'd explode, and it could be anything ranging from inconsequential to significant as to what would trigger his anger and set him off. I sit stiffly in my chair, my heart pounding as I wait in anticipation.

There could be a number of reasons as to what would have him in a bad mood, but usually it was due in part to money lost from gambling. He was constantly gambling, and not just a little bit. He was into everything from card games, sports, horse racing, JaLhi, or some other gambling venture. It was a constant, and he was extreme.

Substantial amounts of money, precious income that could've been used to buy us new shoes, would be forfeited in the name of gambling. When he was on a winning streak, instead of saving the money, or buying practical items with the winnings, he would spend it frivolously. Sometimes we'd eat out every night, and inevitably he'd purchase new sports equipment, like a new baseball bat for three-hundred bucks. He'd find a way to get it if he felt it would advance my brother and me in sports.

On the other hand if I asked him to spend two-hundred dollars on a winter jacket for me, he'd say, "Are you kiddin' me! We'll get one three sizes too big, give it to your older brother first, then after he's done wearing it, you can have it." I'd wait for a couple years before said jacket would get passed down to me, and by then it'd be severely worn. His priorities were interesting to say the least.

The entire family falls deathly silent the second he stops at the edge of table where his dinner plate has been set, ready and waiting for him. In the second he looks down, laying eyes on the Italian bread, his eyes narrow then his jaw muscle ticks, and we knew, it's what always happened, without fail.

In a low muted tone, laced with contempt, he asks, "Why—why would you do that?" I know it's a rhetorical question meant for my mother. Me and my siblings had wanted to ask my mother that very same question earlier today. Even as young kids we knew, we understood his triggers.

He took a deep breath just before he let out a loud explosive roar, heaving the already battered kitchen table up in the air with the strength of a gladiator. At the very same time, I'm having to lean way back in my chair to avoid getting hit by the legs of the table as it gets uprooted from the floor. Then with a loud crash the table comes into contact with the kitchen wall. Spilled drinks, broken dishes, and clanging silverware bounce across the linoleum floor make a cacophony of sounds.

A kaleidoscope of colors mixed with different food textures now decorate the walls and the floor. A single lettuce leaf catches my attention. I watch as it slips off the side of the wall and floats to the ground like a leaf dropping off a tree's limb in the fall. My mother bursts into tears, but that's not enough to get her off the hook, it never is. Crying does nothing but irritate my father all the more. None of us kids move an inch for fear of drawing attention to ourselves. All of us know better than to intervene.

"How many times!" he screams aloud. "Do you think I'm that stupid! Forget about the bread looking different, it tastes different and you know it! Why is it

so damn hard for you to get the right Italian bread?!"
Steam is coming out of his ears now as he begins to
advance on my mother.

My mother cries out and shrinks away, but her
pleas fall on deaf ears. He raises his hands toward her
face, then makes a fist, yelling in Albanian, "You
dummy!"

As my younger sister tears up, my brother and I
exchange a quick glance with each other. Well, my dad
was right about the bread, I think to myself. The
bread from the other bakery was much better, and he
liked it with the seeds on top. This bakery fell short
of his standards, plus they had no seeds on their
bread. My mother knew the deal.

"I was already at the other bakery," my mother
sobs, trying to explain, "I thought I'd just get your
bread there."

"Mondello's is only three doors down from that
bakery!" My father roars. "You were being lazy! Was it
really too much to make just one more stop when you
knew how'd I react?!" We could never understand why
my mother did this, because this was my dad's
reaction every time, without fail. No one could grasp
her mindset or ignorance.

My mother skirts around my father, running off
into their bedroom, crying out loud the entire way.
The door slams behind her, then all falls quiet again. I
watch my father as he takes deep breaths, his chest
heaving, because he's still very angry. He scans over

the floor, taking in the huge mess he made then looks up at my older sister.

"Clean this up," he gruffly tells her as he grabs his jacket then heads back out the door, going God-only-knows where.

I sit here and take in the scene, fixated on the upturned table, taking note of how many dents and dings have accumulated on it. A reflection of the abuse it's taken over the years. There was no keeping count as to how many times this very scenario took place, I just know our kitchen table went through the wall a lot.

Nobody is going to eat dinner tonight, that much I do know. Like I said, it didn't have to be the wrong Italian bread that set him off, he could be just as particular with his salad too. It had to be on the table before he got home without fail, and it had to have tomatoes, cucumbers, and everything else that made up his "perfect" salad, otherwise it had the potential to make him explode.

Of course, his anger management issues didn't always precipitate over food. His short temper could be triggered by anything really, but it usually stemmed from a bad gambling night. Invariably his behavior was justified by the weakest of excuses in order to release the buildup of his frustrations, and it wasn't just the kitchen table that would receive his wrath. He punched his fists through many doors, and every wall in the house. We had holes all over our house. We didn't have any wallpaper on the walls which was a good thing, but that was only because we didn't have the money for it.

~~*

I suppose my father came by his violent tendencies honestly, because my grandfather was a very violent man. He hit his own kids like crazy in their formative years which is exactly where my father got his mindset from. Of course, my grandfather has mellowed out a great deal in his old age, and he never really got physical toward any of his grandchildren. Yes, on occasion my grandfather would get irritated with us and yell, but for the majority of the time, he was wonderful to spend time with.

Having come from Albania, a communist country, my grandparents and parents lived in an environment full of suppression where communicating by physical force went hand in hand with the verbal abuse, especially when it came to child rearing. Violence was a very accepted practice in their culture and it was the norm and very much part of their mentality, and therefore being on the receiving end of it was our norm. It's what they were exposed to, so naturally getting knocked around was very routine and just as common as we breathe air.

In 1938, my father was six years old, and his parents just migrated from Albania. My grandparents came to this country with high hopes of obtaining the all-American dream for their family, or at least be able to give their children a shot at it. The family had initially settled into the lower east side of Manhattan, and to their dismay, found themselves surrounded by a hub of gangsters.

Sadly, my grandparents were doomed from the very beginning as they tried to settle into this new country of theirs. They were subjected to many trials and tribulations, and times were tough, even for the Americans. They didn't have much money, and this obviously added an extra strain to their lives. The fact they spoke little to no English didn't help matters. It was difficult for them to understand much, let alone the new culture and melting pot of people they were immersed in. Everything surrounding them was vastly different than what they were used to. It was like mixing oil and water together, and then expecting them to coalesce.

My father, being so young and trying to fit into his new environment, had a rough time as well, because the absolute moment he set foot on American soil he was bullied. He was already a tough kid, so he took the bullying in stride, and he became very determined to beat the streets.

When my father was in the third grade he decided to quit school and immerse himself in the boxing world. When he did this, he subjected himself to only learning the mentality of the streets, forfeiting his education. In order for him to survive and succeed in his new environment, he recognized quickly that half the battle was not being afraid to fight.

He trained at local gyms and wound up fighting everywhere, trying to make it pro. He was an aggressive fighter who wound up on the Navy boxing team. Back then one didn't need an education to join the military. All one needed was to be able bodied and sixteen. Throughout his boxing career, he was well known for his fighter's jaw. He had the ability to tolerate hits to the head without being knocked out. Either one was born with a jaw like granite or they weren't, it wasn't something a fighter could develop, and no one could take him down because of it. My brother and I were the exact same way.

So when I came along he was determined to train me to beat the streets the exact same way he did… with fearless aggression. He'd always say, "Don't let anyone bully you, or they'll bully you more."

My entire family, cousins included, moved again, buying a house in Woodhaven, Queens. My immediate family shared the second level of a row house while my grandparents lived on the bottom floor. My uncle and his family resided on the very top floor while my other uncle lived in the basement where all our boxing and training took place along with all the equipment stored there.

We also had cousins living on either side of us as well as across the street, but that wasn't enough to shield us from what was transpiring within the city. Unknowingly, my family had exchanged one mob infested hub for another. Queens was just as infiltrated with gangsters as any other suburb in New York. They were in mass numbers everywhere you turned. There was no safe haven.

Some might not believe it, but my father was a very loving and affectionate man. He sacrificed himself for his family and children with an unselfish devotion. The family unit was his mainstay.

He always went out of his way to help others as well, and he was well liked in our community. Everyone who knew my father loved him, enjoyed being with him. The parents in our neighborhood named him King of the Kids, and he was. He was always looking out for the other kids and concerned for their safety as well as ours. He had this gentle side to him, and this particular part of him shined brightly with every kid he ever ran into, including our friends. He devoted his time and energy to the betterment of his kids and community with a passion. If he wasn't coaching my brother and I in boxing, or coaching my baseball teams, he was coaching something else.

I guess he just had tons more patience with the other kids. It was only with his own kids that he was rough and merciless, but everybody in my family loved and respected my dad. It was evident he loved us unconditionally, and with a loyal unwavering devotion to help his children be able to make something of themselves. Unfortunately, because his education took place on the streets, he thought the only way for us to succeed in life was through athleticism.

In my heart and soul, I know beyond a shadow of a doubt, my father did the absolute best he could for his family with what he understood at the time. He was only able to pass down what he, himself, was taught over the years. He wanted us to have a better life than he did, desiring for us to have much success, opportunities, and happiness which was most likely why he rode us so hard.

He also wanted to make an environment where we'd be safe; safe from the perils of the streets. But there was no way he could've foretold that the streets would become far more corrupt and degenerate from when he was a kid. Not even a fortune teller could've foretold that in order to survive in this new reality, one would have to step up their game. The tides were turning before my very eyes, and nobody was aware of the hurricane of violence that was about to fall upon the city.

Chapter 3

At eight years of age, I'm up to 100 push-ups a day and bench pressing 50 pounds. I can fight in the boxing ring like nobody's business, mainly because I have no fear of getting hurt. I've learned how to control the perception of pain early on; I had to. I wasn't allowed to express or display the emotions that accompanied mental distress or physical suffering. I had to control, conceal, restrain, and bottle up these natural instincts that lead to feelings, and every time I did, it would impress my father to no end. I had this innate need to please my father, and I worked hard to gain his admiration. I became a master at repressing any negative emotion he didn't like just to see the look of approval on his face.

I've soaked up every bit of his teachings and stringent standards with the sole intent of mastering them all. I became his little soldier, full of stoicism and loyalty. I wanted to be everything my father wanted me to be and more, and right now, he was on a mission. His plan was for my brother and I to break out and rise above the competition at any cost whether it be in boxing or any other sport.

My dad could give two shits about our feelings, he was after the end result, and he didn't care how he got us there. Granted he went overboard with us much of the time, but I just so happened to thrive in the environment he created for us. I loved the punishing and grueling workouts, and for some reason, I wasn't hypersensitive to the physical or verbal abuse either. Nothing seemed to discourage me from anything, so any challenge my dad placed before me, I embraced it.

I knew I wasn't born with the talent my brother had. I was small and skinny, sloppy in the ring, and I couldn't throw a hook. But I'd walk fearlessly into any fight without thinking twice. I guess this is the only strategy I had at the moment, jump into the fray and take hit after hit, after hit, until I could get better at not only the sport, but fighting in general. It was with this mind-set that made it apparent to all I was never going to give up or stand-down from anything, and when I heard my father say those words with pride, the harder I fought.

My brother on the other hand was born with a natural talent for the sport of boxing. My father loved the way he moved in the ring. He was gifted without even working for it. Graceful and light on his feet was an understatement, and to top it off, he was very quick with his hands. My father would tell him he moved like Mohammed Ali, and although my dad would give him this type of encouragement, in the same breath, he'd dole out the criticism in equal measure. And my brother didn't handle it well. It was the wrong way to motivate my brother.

My dad would arrange boxing matches for us at the house. The purpose of these fights was to coach us, toughen us up, and help us rise above the competition. These fights, of course, would depend on my dad's work schedule so he could be present. School, or any other priorities I had took a back seat to this type of conditioning. It wasn't like a "maybe if I get time to practice or workout today" type schedule, it was a daily regimen he imposed upon us. Some weeks my brother and I were in the ring every single day at the gym.

For us, there was no summer, no winter, there were no seasons, vacations, or breaks. If I didn't practice baseball on top of boxing, or throw the ball against the wall 100 times, I'd be in trouble. And if I wanted to go to the beach with my friends, or to the pool in the hot summer, I had to sneak away to do that, and if my dad found out, he'd be infuriated.

My dad was always looking for a variety of kids with different skill sets for my brother and I to spar with. He'd tell us that the biggest thing in any sport is, "we gotta get in the mix." So we fought different guys of all ages and weight class so we could get better, diversifying our skills, so we could fight kids from all walks of life.

My dad would also tell us, "You can hit the heavy bag all you want. There's a million pro fighters on heavy bag and they all look great. You know why? Because the bag don't hit 'em back." Which brings me to the reason why I can't turn down this coach, or the opportunity to gain more experience.

"Hey Johnny," coach Carmine calls out again, "you wanna get in the ring or not?" he challenges.

I turn around and take a good look at the kid shadow boxing as he dances around in the ring. He's huge, really huge, and he's experienced. He's definitely in a different weight class than me too, and as if reading my mind, the coach adds, "He's getting ready for a fight, but I don't have anyone to spar with him."

"All right," I tell Carmine, "I'll do it." I accept the challenge, because one, I don't back down from anything, and second, I was raised to tough it out. I leave the punching bag swaying in midair behind me as I make my way toward the ring. The closer I get to this kid, the bigger he seems to look. I've seen him in this gym before working out and sparring, and I already know he's too good for me. I'm nowhere near his level of skill in the ring, yet I refuse to renege.

I go ahead and get myself geared up with headgear and gloves while the coach gets in the ring to talk with my new opponent. Each round is set to last for three minutes with one minute rest, just like in a real boxing match. I just hope I'll still be standing after the first round.

A few people start gathering around, wanting to watch the fight which is nothing new to me. Everyone always likes to take a break from their workout to watch.

"Here, let me give you a hand," an older guy says as he comes up beside me. He helps me with the headgear and then tightens the laces up on my gloves. When he's done, I bump my two gloved fists together, testing them out.

"You sure about this?" the guy asks wearily. The look of consternation on his face is evident. He's probably seventeen, but being a seasoned boxer, he knows exactly what's about to go down. "You can still back out," he offers.

I just give him a rough smile and a confident wink. "I'm not a quitter," I assure him. "I'm good."

He purses his lips together as if to stop himself from saying anything more then he looks over at Carmine and shakes his head. Slipping into the ring, I ignore the warning. My adrenaline is already kicking in gear in anticipation of what's to come. I've been involved in so many fights by this point in my life, I'm unfazed. This attitude of mine has been engrained in me from the start; be fearless and never back down from a fight no matter the numbers, or the cost.

My opponent and I bump fists in the middle of the

ring to signal the start of the match. As I walk back to my corner, I stretch my neck from side to side, trying to loosen the tense muscles. The second I turn around to face the center of the ring, coach Carmine shouts out that it's game on.

As usual, I don't hesitate. I just move forward, heading straight into the fight without any grace or skill. I'm just a rough street kid, and this is how I fight. It's the main reason why I'm here at the gym, my father having enlisted the help of a professional trainer. I start dancing on my feet, but it's without any pattern or understanding of anticipating where his first punch is going to come from. A big red glove flashes before my eyes, and then I get slammed by a right hook, quickly followed by left-hand blow to my jaw. Obviously, I'm used to getting hit a lot, and this boy packs a powerful punch, but it does nothing to deter me.

The next strike comes as a short blow to the side of my head causing a sudden loud noise to come through my headgear. My head snaps back just as another jab hits me in the solar plexus.

"Omph!" The breath is stolen from my lungs with a second blow to my gut, but I'm still not going to call it quits. I muster up all my strength somehow managing to land a left uppercut, but that's about the last time I get in a decent punch. The rest of my punches are futile attempts that either do no damage, or don't land. There is no slowing this kid down, and to make matters worse, nobody is here to coach me. I'm left to my own devices, but I don't have a problem with that. I think I was born to fight, because I have zero fear. It's always been natural for me to keep moving forward into the face of danger, even when I probably shouldn't.

I guess I'm considered to be a slow learner, but that's with anything I did growing up. Even when I was learning to ride a bicycle, I wound up hitting about nine or ten trees before I got the hang of it. But once I did learn any skill, I not only excelled at it, I out-shined the rest.

Another blow to the side of my head gets me all twisted around. I stumble and almost fall, but instead I find myself hanging on to the ropes seeing double vision. I shake my head as if that'll help me get my eyesight back. I turn back around with a fierce look of determination. Even though this guy is beating my ass, and I know I've already lost, I won't allow him to get the better of me. At least he's breathing heavily, it means I'm making him work at trying to knock me out.

I dance lightly on my feet, going through the motions in a lame attempt to work my way around him. I should be stalling for time until the round is over, but I don't. The problem with me is I do what I have always done, jump into the thick of it with a vengeance. Even my boxing trainer, Nick has tried to instruct me to be more calculating. He's always telling me, "Every time somebody hits you I want to make sure you hit him back. If he hits you with a jab, you hit him back with a jab, and if he hits you with a right then you hit him with a right."

He was teaching me to counterpunch and this was exactly what I was trying to do in this very situation, but the kid was too experienced for me. He knew how to duck and dodge with speed while being able to pummel me at the same time.

It feels as if these three minutes have turned into ten, and I don't think the end of the round is ever going to get here. Then it's the opposite for our one minute break feeling like I only had a ten second rest.

To be honest, when I fight, the hard blows don't really register, until I take a break. Then there's this immense jolt of pain everywhere, and my brain instantly says, "What the hell just happened, here?!"

I use the back of my forearm to wipe my throbbing nose, and merely glance at the blood coating my arm. I'm more interested in getting a drink of water, but that's not happening. That precious one minute is gone in the blink of an eye, and before I know it the signal to start round two is given.

I'm totally out of breath and getting pummeled left and right. Despite me having headgear on, it hurts like hell to get punched. We're using the fourteen-ounce boxing gloves versus the eight or ten ounce, but it's made no difference. This kid is a power-house and it looks as if he's having too good of a time at my expense while his coach is prompting him on how to give me an early death.

My windpipe is suddenly thick and tight, and I'm not sure what just happened. Something in my neck has started throbbing, and it's not the usual pain... then I realize it's my throat. It's taken me a good two seconds for it to register.

I cough and sputter, but the boy has no mercy on me. I'm getting bashed, whacked, clobbered, and clipped at every turn, yet I still refuse to back down. This second round is probably going to send me straight to the hospital, but I'm too young and stupid to know when to stop. The word doesn't exist for me.

See, one of the things my father did to confuse me was that he sent me mixed messages. He'd yell at me all the time. "Come forward! Come forward." So that's what I did, but in the same breath, he'd say, "But don't get hit a lot." Which is probably pretty laughable right about now.

"Move! Move! Move! Bob and weave... Bob and weave..." I hear my dad's voice, but nothing is registering. My opponent lands a couple more shots, a few that snap my head back and forth several times, and I swear if it wasn't connected to my shoulders my head would've spun around full circle.

I'm probably on the verge of being knocked out, and by the end of the second round, I think I'm going to puke. I don't need a mirror to know I'm a bloody mess. My eyes are nearly swollen shut and I'm feeling weak on my legs. Again, our one minute break seems to last mere seconds before I leave my corner again.

"Get him the fuck outta of the ring!" Vic shouts just before the third round is about to begin. "What the hell are you doing!" he roars at Carmine.

"You just gotta walk into the line of fire, don't you!" Vic yells at me in his thick New York accent. Vic is the one who runs this gym, and he takes his job very seriously. "Where the hell is Nick?"

"He's not here today," I explain to him out of breath. I bend over, resting my hands on my knee caps, trying to catch my breath. As beads of sweat roll off my forehead and drip onto the floor, I notice my sweat is tinged with blood and I begin to wonder just how bad I'm bleeding, or if my nose is broken.

"Well, you're damn lucky I happened to come in when I did, because you don't have the damn sense to quit when you should!"

"And you!" He growls in a low menacing voice, giving Carmine a deathly glare. "You low life scum bag! Don't you ever put my fucking fighter in the ring again! You hear me!" he shouts, his voice having gone from deep and low to booming throughout the entire facility, stopping everyone in their tracks. "He's fucking eight years old! What the fuck were you thinking!?"

He growls, the veins in his neck popping out as he pokes his finger into Carmines chest. It's clear to see Vic is doing everything he can to keep his unspent rage under control. "Don't ever put these kids anywhere, not without me being here!"

I wipe my face down with an already blood-soaked towel then glance over at Carmine, who has nothing to say at the moment, because the guy knows he did wrong. "Just damn you for throwing my fighter in there as a punching bag just so your kid could get some work in!" Vic fires out, his chest heaving as if he was the one who just went through two of the worst rounds of his life. I've seen him mad before, but not quite like this.

If I were to compare my talent level against this kid I was just up against, I would've been given a two on a scale of ten, that's how bad this beating was. And Carmine didn't care that nobody was here to coach me, or have anyone oversee the situation to call it quits if need be, and I didn't know any better. I was totally on my own while Carmine was telling his kid what to do with me the entire time.

But I learned a valuable lesson that day. It was an eye opener as to how much some of these trainers don't give a shit about other kids. It's all about them and what they can do for their fighters; they were merciless, idiot coaches who were okay with throwing unprepared kids into the ring. They didn't care if kids like me got hurt, or if their self-confidence became destroyed because of their abuse.

Lucky for me, this situation only pushed me to want to be tougher, more aggressive and strong-willed, because one day I plan to be the one in control of my own destiny, not allowing anyone to take advantage of me ever again. Nothing will hold me back and no one will be able to control me, and I'll get there using any means necessary.

Chapter 4

My arms are wrapped around the trunk of a tree as if I'm hugging it. I yank at the ropes for the hundredth time, trying to slip my hands out of their binds, but the rope is tied too tightly around both my wrists. With my heart pounding in my chest, I tug frantically, trying to escape. With each hard yank, the twine cuts into my skin deeper and deeper. I already know I'm bleeding around my wrists, but with my adrenaline running so high, I don't even notice it.

It was dusk, and I was on my way home from Forest Park when I was jumped by a man. A very sick man. I didn't even hear him until he bolted out from the dense brush behind me, taking me by surprise. By then, it was too late; he already had ahold of me. With me being so skinny and small, and him being so big and strong, it was a futile fight, but I wasn't going to cave easily. I had stamina and, more than anything, I had the willpower to fight to my last breath.

I wound up with several knocks to the head and a bloody nose before he could wrestle me farther into the thick of the forest to tie me up. I almost got loose a couple times, and the violent scuffle left him winded and uttering countless curse words.

Even if someone could've heard my yells and struggles before he gagged me with a rag that tastes like motor oil, I doubt anyone would've helped. Very few strangers ever step in during a fight unless it involves them.

Fingers slither like a snake on either side of my waist, slipping between the elastic of my jogger pants and my skin. His rough fingertips slide farther downward, removing my pants along the way. I begin to really freak out now, sinking my body against the tree as I try to twist and turn my lower half to get him off me. He crushes the weight of his hard body against my backside, the rough tree bark digging into my stomach. The pressure is so great against me I can't even squirm off to one side anymore.

"Get the fuck off me!" I scream, my words garbled because of the gag.

My sneakers slip against the wet leaves and soft earth, which makes him dig his fingers into my waist even harder to keep me still, and the second his hard male parts press between the cheeks of my butt, I know what he's about to do. My chest goes tight as I grind my teeth against the fabric in lame hopes of being able to slice through it.

Rolling his hips against me, he leans over my shoulder to breathe in low, raspy pants. His hot breath lands on my neck just before his lips press against the pounding pulse in my neck.

I squeeze my eyes shut, willing myself to use my brain, stay calm, and think of a way out of this insanity, instead of being overcome by gripping panic.

I've become desensitized to so much in such a short amount of time in my life, and I've been overexposed to scenes of cruelty and violence, but nothing can compare to this—nothing. This situation never even entered my mind.

It sickens me to know I'm so helpless and so out of control. I've fought against several kids at one time, and I've even been beaten to a pulp, but I still felt as if I was in control.

Being gagged, all I can do is let out low, angered growls, because I refuse to be scared. I'm downright pissed off.

The man lets out a lone groan in response to my vocals, and it reverberates through me in the most sickening of ways. The stench of stale cigarette smoke accosts me, strong and obnoxious. I fight to hold back the vomit that wants to surface, knowing the gag would just make things worse if I puke. I breathe steadily through my nose to avoid the one catastrophe while trying to focus on a way out of the other.

His hand slips around to my front to grope me, and

I flip out even more. "No!" I growl out around the fabric in my mouth, taking deep breaths through my nose.

"Ohh... I like it when the little boys scream and squirm. Makes things more fun," the man teases, the deep tenor of his voice vibrating against my neck. My pulse is jacked so high I can feel my heart beating in my throat. I'm not giving in to this sick man; he will have to kill me first.

There's a rustling in the leaves off to the side, and the man goes stock-still, the muscles of his body stiffening against my backside. He pauses for a moment, trying to decide if the sound was something to be concerned with or not. I make loud growling noises again, hoping there is somebody lurking around and they'll hear me and help.

"Don't go nowhere," the man sardonically chuckles into my ear, and then suddenly the heat from his body against mine is gone. *He's gone for a minute to investigate,* I think to myself, *and this will be my only chance to make a break for it, if I can.*

Knowing each second will count, I work furiously at the ropes, and by the grace of God, somehow, my small wrist is able to slip through one of the binds, releasing me. Immediately taking off in a full run to escape, I don't even look back to see if he's behind me.

Bolting straight up out of bed, I gasp for a breath of air. With my eyes wide open, I grab at my heart. It's hammering like hell in my chest. I quickly take in my surroundings, trying to catch my breath.

Holy shit—what the hell was that? My sheets are soaked, leaving me chilled and clammy. I swallow against the hard lump in my throat and realize it was all a bad dream. I'm safe at home, yet it felt so real.

I look over at my brother, who's still sleeping soundly in his bed while the bright morning sun filters in around the edges of the worn blinds.

I'm still fighting to calm my racing heartbeat, and every time I close my eyes, I can still see the man's face, which does nothing to settle my nerves.

This exact scenario happened to one of my best friends several weeks ago. All I can think is my friend's trauma has been weighing more heavily on me than I thought.

I let out a huge sigh, feeling unusually weak, and I'm taking a guess it has something to do with the nightmare I just had. Either that, or it's the ass kicking I got in the boxing ring yesterday.

The odd thing is, no matter how much physical abuse I take, I'm always able to jump right out of bed, forever on the go and full of fire. So I don't understand what I'm experiencing. I've never let sore muscles or a battered and bruised body slow me down before, because I'm a pro at knowing how to block out the pain.

But today, something is off—different. Maybe it was the nightmare. Then I think of my friend for a moment, knowing he's the one still struggling with the real nightmare. I remember the exact day it happened too, him bolting out of the woods at a full run, trying to get home safely. He's still very freaked out over the incident, and lately, he won't go anywhere in public without someone being by his side. Can't say I blame him, either.

I place my head in my hands and rub at the sides of my temples, hoping to stop the beginnings of a headache from coming on. I force myself to ignore it and get out of bed. As soon as I do, I wish I hadn't, because I collapse back on the mattress, the room spinning.

I know I got hit in the head a lot yesterday, but this is ridiculous. It's as if all the blood in my body is moving at a snail's pace, making me sluggish. I carefully get up this time, determined to shake it off, figuring if I just move around, I'll feel better. Being only eight years old, there's no way for me to understand what's happening to me.

Maybe all those blows to my head did more damage than I thought. I guess that's why my dad went ballistic when he found out about what happened. If I thought Vic was mad, my father was infuriated about the unfair sparring match. All my father wanted to do was go kick Coach Carmine's ass, and I believe he just might.

I've got a busy day ahead of me; I don't have time to be sick, knowing I'll lose my turn in the one bathroom our family shares if I procrastinate. That one bathroom in our one-floor apartment means my parents, brother, two sisters, and I all have to share. It becomes very inconvenient at times, especially when my sisters drag their feet.

I slowly make my way to the bathroom, my head pounding with each step I take. Sliding the shower curtain out of the way, I reach in and start the water. The effort it took to get this far cost me a great deal of energy.

By the time I'm done using the toilet, I become lightheaded and dizzy, but I push past it and step into the shower's spray. I'm halfway done washing up when suddenly I turn hot and flushed. It's an uncomfortable sensation, like a cold sweat radiating off my neck, making me jittery and clammy.

Ugh! I can't figure out what's happening to me. I wipe at my neck with the back of my hand to find it slimy to the touch. Frustrated, I adjust the shower's temperature to spray cooler water over my body. I can't afford to be sick. I've got a baseball game this afternoon. Quickly, I do the math in my head as to how many hours I have to get myself together before game time.

I hurry and finish up with my shower so I can go back to bed and lie down until this sickness passes, but then I get sidetracked by a wave of dizziness. It's so severe my hands instinctively slap themselves against the slick shower wall in order to steady myself.

Closing my eyes, I lift my chin as I let the cool water rain onto my face, hoping to get rid of this bizarre feeling that's overtaking me. It's as if a locomotive is running through my head, giving me this spaced-out aura.

All of this sickness comes to a climax, plowing through my body like a cyclone. My knees buckle out from underneath me as I make a lame attempt to grab the shower curtain to help keep me on my feet, but it doesn't work. All my muscles go slack, and the shower curtain and the rod come crashing down over top of me. Then, everything goes black.

"Mutin! Mutin!" my dad curses frantically in Albanian as I slowly come to. The water pelting down on the plastic curtain sounds like a monsoon in a rainforest before it comes to a halt. The plastic crinkles as my dad swiftly pushes aside the curtain, trying to get to me. His strong arms slip underneath my soaked and limp body as he scoops me up, lifting me out of the tub. "Del!" he calls for my mother.

Through my foggy haze, her voice goes shrill as she cries out, "oh zot e ka mbulu gjaku," which means, "oh my God, he's covered in blood." I don't understand what she's talking about. I don't remember seeing any blood. Nobody knows what just happened or understands what this means for me. They're just as confused as I am.

My limbs flop all over the place like a rag doll as my father shifts me in his arms to get a better grip. "Më jep një peshqir," he orders my mother to get him some towels over and over in his native tongue. I'm guessing he's repeating himself in order to keep my mother focused and on task. His tactic appears to have worked, because within seconds, I've got soft cotton towels all around me.

My father carries me out into the living room, where he lays me down on the sofa. Blankets now cover my body while my dad wraps my head with a towel. He works quickly to get my skull wrapped, all the while applying pressure to the side of my head. Seems like the more pressure he applies, the more thumping and throbbing takes place in my head, but I don't complain or utter a sound. I block out the pain.

"What's going on, Meti?" my grandmother asks, anxiety lining her voice. Her eyes widen the second they land on the blood-soaked towel wrapped around my head. Her hand flies to her chest as if I might be giving her a heart attack, but I'm too wiped out to tell her I'm fine. That would be a flat-out lie, but I don't like seeing her unsettled like this.

"I heard a loud crash. I yelled out, 'Johnny? Johnny?'" my dad explains in Albanian. "But no answer. Then I bang on the door, and still no answer." Hearing all of this come from my dad's shaken voice seems crazy, because he never gets distressed, but I've got the banged-up head to prove it. "And when I open the bathroom door, he's lying on the shower floor. His arms and legs wouldn't stop jerking. He was like a fish out of water. Then blood—blood everywhere!" he exclaims, his voice on edge. "Blood, all over the tub, all over his face." I can't imagine what was running through his mind when he found me lying in the bottom of the tub, violently convulsing for what seemed like hours when it was only minutes. "He fell, hit his head on the water faucet."

My dad turns back to me, giving me a worried look, and as he stays by my side, my mom and grandmother wear a hole in the floor as they pace back and forth. After a while, my father unwraps the towel from around my head to inspect the damage. "Bleeding has stopped," he tells me, and then he rewraps my head, appearing a little more relaxed now that he's got the bleeding under control. He looks me in the eye, and asks, "You good now, son?"

"I think so," I tell him, even though my head hurts, but I'm totally wiped out from the ordeal. I always want to make my dad proud of me, even now, despite having no control over what just happened. I want him to know I can tough it out.

"Oh—Bebi im." Hearing my grandmother's soft, distinct voice from behind my dad relaxes me. Her heartfelt emotion can always be felt with each word she breathes, "Oh zemra ime," she continues to repeat, "oh my heart" in Albanian as she fidgets with worry.

As soon as my dad is satisfied I will be fine, he stands up, at which time my grandmother immediately slips into his place to sit beside me.

She takes stock of my situation for herself, running the back of her fingers tenderly over my cheek. "You look so pale, my *shpirti*," she whispers. My grandmother always speaks with so many Albanian endearments, and I love to hear them all, shpirti especially which means 'my life', or 'my soul'. I'm completely drained, and just want to sleep, but I manage a small smile for her.

"*Te dua,*" she whispers, telling me she loves me as she leans forward to give me a gentle kiss on my forehead. "Can I get you anything, *shpirti?*"

"Tired," I tell my grandmother, too exhausted to even try to explain how I feel.

"Okay, you rest," she says. "I will be here when you wake up."

My grandparents are my guardian angels. They were always very prevalent throughout my entire life, but in my younger years, they basically raised me, and at certain times, I felt closer to them than my own parents.

Much of this was due to the fact my mother went to work when I turned six. Her job was a point of contention with my father, but eventually, she won out. My father, however, was gone far more often than anyone. When he wasn't at home, he was either out driving his taxi or gambling.

For the most part, I wound up raising myself, going unsupervised much of the time. I can't blame my parents, they had to work, and when the weekends came they were busy with their own lives. I don't think they knew any better, because they were so young themselves.

But little did any of us know, I had just experienced my very first full-blown epileptic seizure.

These types of episodes would happen several more times before my parents caught on to the fact I needed to see a doctor. I guess they were finally able to put two and two together, making a correlation between me having always fallen over everything, crashing into glass tables and down the stairs, my entire childhood. All of us thought maybe I was just clumsy, tripping over my own two feet. But the first memorable seizure I experienced was at the age of five. I didn't know what happened, nobody did, and I didn't know how to describe what I was experiencing. I was in school going down a set of steps, and then suddenly, I blacked out. It was a nasty fall, with me tumbling down headfirst.

One would think today's dramatic event would've constituted a trip to the emergency room, but not for our family. When things of this nature would happen, we'd just deal with the issue at hand then tough it out. So that is exactly what I did—toughed it out.

It would take a couple more years before I'd be diagnosed with epilepsy. It took even longer to understand there was a serious correlation between getting knocked in the head repeatedly during fighting and boxing, and all the detrimental side effects it would have on my body, which would trigger these epileptic seizures. That knowledge would come at a price too— my price—and it would be out of my control.

Chapter 5

I'm not quick enough to step out of the way and evade my brother as he rams straight into my front like a linebacker going in for a quarterback sack. The wind gets knocked out of me as I'm propelled backward. I'm half expecting my body to collide against the living room wall upon impact, but that never happens, and before my brain can register what's going on, I'm still traveling through the air.

The distinct sound of glass exploding surrounds me, and it's not until it feels like a sledgehammer has been smashed against my back that I realize I've been forced through a closed window.

With it all happening so fast and finding myself in a free-fall, I barely even have time to register that I'll soon land on the hard ground two stories down. I gasp for air, bracing for severe impact, ready to have the air stolen from my lungs, but it never comes. What I do come into contact with are the roof shingles that line the roof of the ground-floor front porch. Shards of glass rain down on me like a hailstorm.

The roof I've landed on is not flat—it has a pretty decent incline—but it's enough to break my fall, giving me the opportunity to twist my body around and grab onto the rough surface to keep me from rolling over the edge of the roof.

There's glass everywhere, glittering in the sun like an exposed mine of diamonds. I look down and exhale in relief. I'm covered in tiny glass fragments from my hands to my feet. A few sharp slivers are piercing into my backside, but mostly my hands as I grip the roof like my life depends on it.

"You just slammed me through the window!" I look up, shouting at my brother in disbelief. He looks at me for a moment, and once he realizes I'm fine, so to speak, he takes stock of the broken window and I already know what's running through his head. "Dad is going to kick your ass for this," I tell him, pissed off.

His attention snaps back to me with a rebuttal on his lips. "You are every bit as much a part of this as me."

"The hell I am." Even though I say this, I know different. It doesn't matter who's at fault; both my brother and I will take the fall for any damage done. "I could've fallen off the roof and broken my neck, asshole."

When Jimmy and I fought, we fought really hard. They were not like regular sibling fights; we took things to the extreme.

Once I get my equilibrium back, I decide not to climb back through the window in which I smashed. I slide down to the edge of the roof on my stomach and do a free hang. My feet dangle in the air as I glance down over my shoulder, figuring I've got about a five-foot drop. I let go and land on the ground with ease then carefully brush the glass off me.

My brother comes bolting out the front door—not so much to check on me, but to assess what the damage looks like from the outside. He looks up at the second story window in deep thought, and I can already hear what he's thinking.

"What kind of story are we going to come up with this time?" he asks.

My older sister appears, popping her head out from between the broken glass shards and the nearly empty window frame. "Ohh, you're in trouble," she sing-songs.

"Don't tell him," we both plead out of some sort of sick hope that my sister will be able to keep her mouth shut, but it's not likely. If it's not my sister ratting us out to my father, it will be my mother.

My brother looks up, and asks, "Why do you have to tell him these things? You know he's going to come home and beat us up."

Jimmy and I get the glass all cleaned up. We find some clear plastic and duct tape in the basement so we can create a makeshift window to help keep the elements out. The last step is to draw the curtains shut in hopes of it never being discovered. An out of sight, out of mind type thing.

By the time my mother comes home from work, it's my younger sister who cannot keep her mouth shut. When my mother finds out about the window, she begins screaming at us. It's a ceaseless chant, voiced with bitter frustration that she can't control us. The fact she couldn't control us is one of the reasons we'd been fighting all day and night.

Usually, her method of discipline would involve trying to hit us with a hanger or something—she almost always had a hanger in her hand, swinging it as us. The problem was, she'd get even more infuriated, because she could never get in a good whack. The vast majority of her attempts to beat us with a clothes hanger was in vain, because either my brother or myself would be too fast for her. Normally, we'd be able to grab the hanger from her hands, or we'd just simply take off and run, with her yelling at us from behind.

Oddly, she doesn't choose the infamous hanger tonight, but she does pull out her main weapon: using the threat of our father.

"You wait until your father comes home!" she screams at us. He was always made aware of our misbehaving before he got home for the night. He'd call home several times throughout the day and evening to check in with everyone. No matter where he was—out gambling, or driving his cab—he was like clockwork with the calls. We'd beg our mother not to tell him, especially if we knew ahead of time that he lost big on his gambling bets, but she didn't care. She had no mercy when it came to my brother and me catching a good beating.

My mother would put us on the phone with him when we were acting up, and he'd typically say in a low threatening tone, "I am telling you right now—when I get home, you're gonna get a beating. So you'd better be waiting for it."

True to his word, it's 3:00 a.m. when I'm yanked out of bed. Half awake, I can see through the dimly lit room that my brother is already standing by the edge of his bed, awaiting punishment. This wasn't an unusual occurrence for my dad to come home in the middle of the night to wake us up and beat the crap out of us for the day's transgressions.

Dammit. I was hoping he would've won big money tonight, which would've invariably put him in a good mood. If that happened, there was a good chance he wouldn't hit us at all. There were times when he was in a really great mood, and we didn't get punished. He was known to call us sometimes around dinnertime and order us not to tell our mother, but for my brother and me to meet him on the corner up the street. He would then take us to a Mets game at Shea Stadium, my mother thinking the entire time that he was at work. He did this quite a bit. She would have no clue where my brother and I had taken off to until we all got home at eleven at night.

But honestly, it was like torture, having to wait for hours on end until he got home, leaving us on pins and needles and wondering the entire time what the fallout would be. It was always a hit or miss with him, and it would all depend on the outcome of his gambling. One thing we never had to question ourselves with was whether or not he was in a bad mood. We could tell from the moment we laid eyes on him. And tonight, he was in a very bad mood.

Chapter 6

Living in and among such a complex structure of debasement, corruption, and a sordid society, I wasn't thinking about things being right or wrong as a kid. I was just doing, and in many cases, I felt as if justice was being served whether I was directly involved or not. I developed my own ethical codes of conduct through watching my father, and with time, I learned how to justify anything.

Each significant event that unfolded before me in my formative years, ones that forced me to confront them head on, had slowly molded and shaped me as a person along with my perceptions of the world like a ball of soft clay. So, by the time I became a teenager, that clay had then hardened, having turned into a resistant and mighty slab of stone, and I was no longer flexible. That's who I was. I became a force to be reckoned with.

~~*

My dad sits down beside me at the kitchen table the second my mother leaves out the door for work. I'm focused on trying to scarf down my bowl of cereal for breakfast, because I'm already running late for school. My dad's bright blue eyes sparkle with mischief. I know that look. I smile around my spoon, as he leans in to tell me in a conspiratorial whisper, "Around noon, go to the nurse's office and say you're feeling sick."

Usually, I get a heads-up the day before, including all the details, but I guess something has come up at the last minute.

"Where are we going?" I ask excitedly.

"There's a card game in Yonkers," he explains. "We'll meet up at our usual spot. I'll be there around noon waiting for you."

I swallow my mouthful of food and nod. "Okay."

My father would always pull me out of school to go gambling with him. It was the norm, and my mother hated it. Hence the reason why he waited until she left to go to work. Even though she has no say in family affairs, it's still in everyone's best interest, especially hers, for my parents not to argue about it. It never ends well.

I get up and put my bowl in the sink, wearing a grin the whole time. From the age of five, it was my dad who taught me how to be a hustler. I love the excitement of going gambling with him, and I can't even begin to describe how it makes me feel to know I'm my father's first choice when it comes to being his partner.

My father's life has always revolved around sports and gambling; therefore, mine does too. Point blank, my father is a pathological gambler, highly addicted. Of course, I didn't know this until later in life, because I was groomed to be his sidekick from the very beginning, and I knew nothing different.

He was constantly taking me with him to card games, horse races, and sporting events of every kind. If he could place bets, he was doing it. Sometimes, we'd go to card games that lasted all night long, starting from ten at night and going nonstop until six the next morning. It was a constant adrenaline rush for me. There were no specific gambling days carved out for staking his money on something. It was whenever he knew something was going on, and the time of day or year didn't matter. It was year-round and constant.

The thing about my father, despite him not finishing elementary school, he was extremely intelligent and a master with numbers. He not only knew how to count cards with his eyes closed, but he knew how to beat every system out there. Being charismatic came natural to him, and he was so good at what he did that he was able to sway and corrupt both dealers and athletes alike. Since I had been exposed to all the tricks of the trade, diligently watching and learning over the years, I knew how all of it was done.

I guess you could say he taught me everything I needed to know in order to survive the streets, including how to manipulate games, money, and people. As early as age nine, it was a thrill knowing that someone as young as me could have the edge on unsuspecting gamblers.

I learned the easiest way to get sent home from the nurse's office was to say I was feeling dizzy. The nurse would inevitably call my father at home, and he would insist they let me leave, because of my epilepsy. Sometimes, they'd give me a look of skepticism, but really, what could they do? Nothing.

By the time I fake my way out of the nurse's office and meet my dad on the corner beside the school, it's 12:15 p.m.

I open the passenger door to his big white Caddy and slide into the front seat. "How'd it go?" he asks.

"Not a problem," I respond with a smile, ready for some excitement. We talk about sports on the way to Yonkers while occasionally reviewing our signals.

We have to go to these private clubs, for several reasons, but the main one being I'm not allowed in legitimate establishments because I'm underage.

We pull into a rundown garage and find a parking space then make our way to the front entrance. The entryway door is chipped with aged, peeling blue-grayish paint, looking as if it should've had a fresh coat ten years ago. To my surprise, when we enter the place, it turns out to be decently clean and sizable, not as shabby as I had initially expected it to be. From the outside, the building is deceiving and looks much smaller than it actually is.

I take in the scene through the smoke-filled room and dingy lighting. Many men are drinking over their lunch hour, which works to our advantage most of the time. My dad never drinks; he always wants his wits about him. I trail behind my dad, who's dressed in casual attire, dress pants and shoes and a white T-shirt under his sweater.

He nods to a few people he knows, and there are a few faces I recognize. My dad, having grown up on the streets, knows an exorbitant amount of people from all walks of life, but the majority of them are gangsters. He was a tough guy with his hands; he wasn't a killer, but he wasn't afraid of these men either. Everyone liked my dad, which made me all the more proud to be his son.

I've been exposed to the mafia and backroom gambling deals from the very beginning. None of us have a real fear of gangsters or mob affiliations. Many of these guys have either been our friends for years, or close acquaintances.

My uncle, Harry, is a big gambler, his partner a wise guy and a cousin of Lucky Luciano. My other uncle, Mike, lives downstairs with my grandparents. He's a gangster too, and when I say gangster, I mean a killer. Sadly, he's living with us because he's dying of cancer, and my grandparents are helping to take care of him.

"Hey, Matt," Red calls out to get my dad's attention from one of the poker tables. Wearing the typical and trendy plaid jacket and fedora of our era, Red was just another gambler who hit all the spots we did. Though they hadn't spent any amount of time together to speak of, he and my dad go way back, having grown up together. My dad smiles and gives Red a cordial nod. This place is like any other backroom private gambling club. It's a large, wide-open single room with several tables of games going on at the same time.

I get a soda from the bar in the back of the room from the bartender then begin operating incognito by acting like the normal boy I am—bouncing with energy and unable to sit still. My father takes up residence at one of the tables, and I recognize that as my cue to find a place to get settled near his table but stay out of way. It's game time. I pay close attention to him the entire time, looking for certain signals from him to tell me when my work begins.

My father knows where to count cards, and where not to. He never puts us at risk by counting cards or hustling gangsters. We are only here to target the so-called suckers. For us, they're easy to pick out. It was obvious to even me when someone didn't understand when to fold their hand or when to double up. My father knows how to read them, because they don't press for more money when their cards are hot, and they don't know how to bluff the poker table.

I was surrounded not only by watching and playing sports myself, while having an unforgiving training schedule all year round, but I was also being primed to learn how to gamble in every game imaginable, taking part in all my father's schemes.

Amazingly, he was able to count cards, scope out, and scam other card players, and then, as if that weren't enough, he had the charisma to sway the dealers. Only after a relationship was forged, when he felt they could be trusted, would he then approach these dealers with the intent of buying them off.

Before I turned seven, I watched and learned firsthand from my father how things were done in the gambling world. He was a genius, not only having a vast amount of knowledge with stakes and wagers, but he also understood how to read people and situations, manipulating them to his advantage.

My father's abilities to persuade people into being part of his schemes, however, went far beyond cards. Jockeys and sportsmen from all walks of life were evaluated with diligence on a constant basis as to whether or not they would make great allies.

When my father was counting cards, he never put us at risk by doing so while gangsters were around.

To these men at the poker table, I'm just an innocent, ignorant kid who knows nothing about cards, and me being small for my age makes me appear that much younger. These men probably think my dad simply wanted to stop in to play a few hands but was left with the unfortunate chore of babysitting me today. What they don't realize is I know how to play all these games and much more.

The dealer shuffles the cards then passes them out to the players with skilled practice. I wind up sitting on a stool on the opposite side of the table from my father, eating a snack and drinking a soda, looking around as if I'd rather be somewhere else. I let the men get in a couple rounds of cards before I spring into action.

With all the players being heavily engrossed in their game, too busy to take notice of me, I start to slowly maneuver around the game table while getting quick glimpses of their cards. As I stand behind one particular man, I nonchalantly turn away and touch my head as my fingers slide down my face, signaling to my dad that he's holding a pair of face cards. All these signals are ones my dad came up with. They're exactly like all the baseball signals I've learned by playing the sport, so these signals are easy for me to remember.

I glance over another man's shoulder, who's sitting beside the dealer. I'm able to give another successful signal that goes unnoticed. I rub my forearm for a brief second as if I have an itch, telling my father the man is holding a pair. If the guy had two pairs, I'd rub one arm then the other. This is the most exciting part of the game for me, the challenge of having the upper hand and not getting discovered. There are times when we've had some close calls, but all of this gets my blood racing and heart pounding, making me feel alive.

A waitress, who is in barely-there attire, approaches me with a drink in her hand. Her corset is so tight I think her breasts are going to spill out of the low-cut lace and leather any second. I blink several times, unable to remove my gaze from her chest. Her long jet-black hair is smooth, shiny, and straight and must go halfway down her back.

She leans in and gives me an endearing grin, her long lashes and bright blue eyes holding me captive. I'm frozen—speechless and unable to move. As if she understands my dilemma, she unwraps my fingers from my empty glass to replace it with a new soda. She turns and walks away, and the view of her backside is just as gorgeous as her front. I hear my dad laughing out loud, which pulls me back into the moment. I shift my eyes his way to see he's shaking his head at me in amusement.

"You like gawking at that big-chested waitress," he states with a wide smile, purely entertained by my reaction. My mouth is dry. I swallow around the lump in my throat and remember to breathe. Holy hell, she was a looker. My dad gives me a playful wink as I pull myself back together.

I refocus on the card game and take small sips of my soda. I pay attention to the players, their reactions, and who's winning the most. After a few hands, I have a good guess who our target will be.

Not too long after, it's as I suspected; my dad singles out the very man I've been keeping an eye on. He motions to me with a cryptic gesture, confirming it. He's an older man wearing a brown hat, and he's been nursing his drink while smoking a cigar for the past ten minutes. He's pegged as the one to beat... the one who appears to have the hot hand tonight. Therefore, he becomes my main objective. I take a drink of soda as I casually move around the table until I wind up standing behind the broad-shouldered man. The guy is holding his cards close to his chest, which is driving me nuts. I'm forced to inch up behind him, little by little, in order to get a good read on his cards. I have to get so close to this man's backside I can see the hairs sticking out of his ears.

A few hours pass in the blink of an eye, and everything appears to be running smoothly. I've watched the waitress as she flirts with my dad several times. I really can't blame this waitress for being drawn to him. He's in excellent shape, not an ounce of fat on him, and truth be told, he's a very handsome guy. Plus, the icing on the cake is he has that unusual charisma about him. Just the mere fact of him being in the room, he exudes this energy that catches so many people's attention. I guess the waitresses likes my dad, because he tips well. He always comes across to people as having money to spend, which is one of the main keys to attracting beautiful yet loose women who prided themselves on being someone's arm candy. It's all par for the course, especially if that's what a guy is looking for on top of gambling. But my dad isn't looking for that—he's looking to win.

We've been here for several hours now, and I rub at my jawline. Yet another secret signal to my father. With my little gesture, my father then returns his own all-too-familiar signal, telling me we're in the final round. This is it; he's going in for the kill, and this means we hope to walk away with it all, because he's going to be anteing up the pot.

The noise of gentlemen's chatter fades away from me as I focus on the most important hand of the night. Maybe my dad has lost a couple hundred dollars by this point, I'm not sure, but he's acting the part of an everyday gambler to the T. He loses some hands in order to keep everyone from suspecting anything.

I send more clandestine signals and pretend not to watch as men add more money to the center of the table. My father has been working hard at building up the pot, and from the looks of things, I'd bet there's a couple grand sitting on that table for some lucky winner. The player I've had my eyes on most of the night exchanges out a couple cards, and at a quick glance, I touch my head, indicating the man has a pair of aces.

When it comes time to call everyone's hands, and each man lays down their cards face up, I realize immediately by the look on my father's face that I screwed up somewhere along the way. I know that face. Like a boiling teakettle, he's steaming on the inside. The telltale sign he's most famous for when he's irate is when he puckers his lips, which is exactly what he's doing right now. He has to hold his composure though. The other players at the table are merely thinking he's upset because he lost his hand, but I know differently.

I didn't give him the right signal. The man with the cigar pulled triple aces, and I should've seen it. But sometimes, it's hard to see all the cards at all times. I'd swear on my life he only had two pairs.

I glance at my dad, and I'm very aware of the fact that, if he could get up right now, he'd crack me over the head. But he can't, or he'll give himself away. Like a pulled pin on a hand grenade, there will be an inevitable explosion coming my way. There is no doubt I'm going to get a clobbering after this game.

His heated glare bores into me. He's looking at me like, *You fucking moron! What the fuck is wrong with you?* He doesn't even need to say the words. I can already hear him yelling at me in his deep voice. It's reverberating through my head with sobering clarity.

If I could pull us out of this, save the day and have him walk away ahead, it would mean he'd win for the night. This would make him very happy. It'd curb his anger to where he might not even be pissed off. If he walked away a winner for the night and had a good time, he always stopped and got us something to eat at a restaurant.

I've pulled us out of many screw-ups before, but this particular game is over and there is no fixing this one or being able to break even. He's lost big, and I am doomed to face his wrath.

This is my life, a roller coaster of ups and downs. I sit here and think about my dad and the times he comes home broke, and the bad mood it puts him in. The odd thing with him... even broke, he'd stop and give some bum on the street ten dollars. If he had a twenty, he still give them ten dollars, but if that's all he had on him was a ten-dollar bill, he'd give them the entire ten. I had come to learn he had no rhyme or reason when it came to money. He was forever all over the place with his fortunes, or lack thereof. It all depended on what his priorities were in that moment in time. He had so many unusual ways about him. He was hard to figure out, but I loved him just the same.

When he would win big, he would constantly take us out to eat dinner as a family. He'd take us to so many places, but we never went on any vacations, because crazily enough, we didn't have money. His money management was lacking, to say the least, but to my father, vacations were a waste of time. He'd say,

"We don't need to go anywhere."

The family would all counter with, "We'd like to go to the beach."

"What?" he'd ask, perplexed. "You want to go to the beach, you go for the day."

I agreed with some things he believed in, but not all of them. Certain things he said made sense to me. For example, when someone was buying a headstone for a burial, his argument was, "Are they kiddin' me? Spending ten to twenty-thousand for a concrete plaque to put in a cemetery? It's a con."

All the men at the table laugh out loud at something, catching my attention. I watch my father as he bows out of the game gracefully, shaking everyone's hand with a false smile as he says goodbye. I follow behind as we make our way out the door. He remains quiet the entire way to the car, but I can sense the rage within him, and it wants to burst out.

He slips into the driver's seat as I get in on the passenger side of the car. As he starts the car and pulls out onto the main street to take us home, his lips are still pursed tightly together. The car is deathly quiet, but after we go through a few more stoplights, he finally blows his top. He hits the dashboard hard and fast with his fist, making a horrendous sound. My dad has punched that dashboard so many times over the years that I'm surprised it's not in pieces by now.

"Where was your fuckin' head?" he screams at the top of his lungs, as he slaps the dash again and again.

"It's no different from baseball. You just got to follow the signals!"

Most kids, even abused kids, would probably want to shrink back into the car seat and disappear, but I'm so used to him yelling and hitting it doesn't phase me.

"What did you want me to do, Dad?" I ask in self-defense, not in the least bit intimidated.

"Pay fucking attention!" he roars, and then adds another heavy-handed punch to the dash. "Why aren't you paying attention?"

"I was paying attention," I argue back. "I'm always following the signals."

"No!" he yells, shaking his head. "No, you weren't. You were thinking of something else. What were you thinking about?"

"I swear, I was thinking about cards, Dad. I didn't see the third ace!" I respond firmly, full of confidence.

"This is a job, Johnny! We're partners!"

My dad would always say that, and despite him yelling, cursing, and hitting at me the entire way home, I smile on the inside, because he sees me as his partner. As dysfunctional as our lives are, we're blood, and the two of us have an inseparable bond, making us one. There's a deep-seated love for my dad, which surpasses all, with respect and loyalty engraved on my soul.

Chapter 7

"**K**eep that damn bracelet on!" my father screams at me as I'm halfway out the door. I'm supposed to wear this silver bracelet that has an encryption written in red bright, bold letters, *EPILEPTIC*. It's all I could do to wear this stupid thing for a month. I hated people seeing me with it on.

The door creaks loudly on its hinges as I shut the front door behind me with a loud, unintentional boom. "And stop slamming the doors!" Dad yells out after me, but that too falls on deaf ears. I'm already halfway down our front walkway as I take off the burdensome bracelet and chuck it into the unused empty lot next door to our house.

I don't even give it a second thought, as I'm entirely focused on what mischief will materialize for me and my friends today. All my friends are waiting at the dead-end part of my street. The sun is shining brightly, and even at eight in the morning, the humidity is thick with the summer's heat. I love my summers. It's when I consider myself the freest, being able to leave the house in the early morning and not having to come home until the streetlights turn on. Of course, that was only to touch base and eat dinner before taking off again, usually to play a game of Ring-A-Leerio when it was dark.

There were so many deaths in our area that everyone nicknamed our little community Deathhaven, instead of using its actual name, Woodhaven. The deaths weren't only caused from all the murders and drugs, but from everything you could think of. One guy in our neighborhood became a fireman and died in a fire. Another from cancer. It was never-ending, one death after another, and it bred a lot of heartache in our little community. These circumstances are things a child shouldn't be a witness to at such a young age, but at the time, I thought this was the norm.

Besides being a mostly white neighborhood, we're still a melting pot, coming from many different countries. The majority in our area is mainly comprised of Irish. We also have German, Spanish, and a few Italians sprinkled in here and there.

Because of certain events and tragic incidents that took place over the years within our community, our neighborhood banded together to support one another. We have become so close knit and very protective of each other, and in many ways, I'm considered extended family to many of them.

Everything circled around one or two blocks of my house—the J-train, elementary schoolyard, Franklin Lane High School, Forest Park, local stores, and my friends.

"Where is everybody?" I ask as I approach my two good friends, Joey and Charlie.

"They're already waiting for us," Joey says, waving his hand toward the school.

"Well, let's go," I tell them as I walk toward the fence that we cut a hole in last year so we could slip through the wires. Our mission: to hang out in the schoolyard and goof off. My elementary school was PS 97, and on the far side of the grounds is where Kevin and Timmy live. Even though they are brothers, all of us got along great.

As we approach our meeting place, I can tell already by the number of kids we have waiting on us what kind of game we're going to play. "Johnny on the Pony?" Timmy calls out with a warm smile as we get closer.

Jerry, our other friend, gives a curt nod as he reaches into his pocket and pulls out a quarter. He flips it high, and when the coin is midair he calls out, "Heads."

I lunge forward and grab the coin out of the air and then slap it down on the back of my hand, wearing a devious grin. I pull my hand away to reveal the face of the coin. "Heads, buddy," I tell him.

I'm the first one who gets picked by Jerry to be on

his team. I usually am, but my friends and I always try to get on the same team. Despite me being a skinny kid, I'm unusually strong for my age, but I also have something most kids don't—a strong determination to win and hold my ground no matter what. I step over to the side and stand behind Jerry as each team captain takes turns choosing who they want on their side, until we're divided up into two equal teams.

Of all the games, Johnny on the Pony is probably one of the most dangerous to play, causing the most injuries, but it's also what happens to the losers that gets downright violent in nature. We're mischievous boys, full of unspent adrenaline, and if I have to guess, part of it too is to prove to the next kid how tough one can be.

The kids on my side are goofing off and talking while the last few kids are being divvied up. There's a new kid on my team I haven't seen before, but nevertheless, he has the guts to cut in on our conversation and ask me, "What the hell's wrong with your voice?"

I stare at him like he has two heads and narrow my eyes. "Nothin'," I reply matter-of-factly.

As I size the kid up, he appears a couple years older than me, but he's nothing I can't handle. "Well, you sound like a frog," he says with a half-snigger.

"Shut the fuck up," I tell him in my hoarse voice. I couldn't care less what anyone thinks of my voice. It doesn't bother me, but I'm not going to be made fun of either.

Charlie interrupts, trying to persuade the new kid to shut up. "I wouldn't mess with him if I were you," he warns, shaking his head.

Immediately, the older boy holds up both his hands in surrender. "Sorry, was just curious," he tells me in an apologetic tone. I stare him down, giving him a cold glare. He repeats his apology, so I let it go. Nobody knows why my voice is hoarse. At first, the doctors thought it was throat cancer. I'm only a kid and I didn't smoke, so they were perplexed. After doing all kinds of medical testing, including having scopes placed down my throat, the doctors came to the conclusion that I was constantly straining my vocal chords. They attributed this froggy voice not to something physical, but to all the mental stresses I was living under.

"Ready?" Charlie asks, slapping me on the back.

"Yeah," I tell him, as our team of twelve begins to form a straight, narrow line, positioning ourselves one kid behind the other. At the same time, we all bend forward at the waist, leaning our upper body onto the person's back who's in front of us, while wrapping our arms tightly around their waist. By the time we're all connected, we resemble a long human caterpillar.

As the other team lines up about fifty feet behind us, we all hold onto each other with a death grip, bracing ourselves for some seriously heavy weight to pile on top of our backs. I tuck my head down and to the side in hopes of avoiding getting kicked in the face, or worse. The other team's goal is to jump on our backs as hard as possible, trying to collapse our line, which is called the Pony. Over time, if these kids got really good, they'll be able to jump over bodies as far forward as they like, strategizing where they think our weakest link will be.

"Ready?" someone calls out from behind us.

My entire team calls back in unison, "Ready." We all know the first person to jump on us is going to get a good running start so he can basically Leap Frog himself across our backs. I close my eyes tightly, bracing for the impending impact.

The entire line of our human caterpillar lunges forward as the first guy lands heavy and hard about two people behind me. A few grunts surface from our line, and not three seconds later, the process repeats itself. By the time the seventh person has landed on top of his own men, piling the weight on, they look like the Leaning Tower of Pisa while trying to cling to each other on top of our unstable foundation.

I've been elbowed five times already, and all I can hear are grunts and strings of curse words being uttered, both from above and from our own team. All we can hope for, as they pile themselves on top of us, is that one from the other team will fall off our backs. If that's the case, we'll win, but so far, everyone is holding steady.

The middle section of my team has taken the

brunt of the weight this time, and luckily, I'm not in the middle of it. I almost want to laugh at the absurdity of this game, especially when someone yells out, "Jerkoff! You're squashing my balls!" My shoulders begin to shake as I fight to hold in the laughter. If I give in to the hysterically funny situation, I'll fall down, because right now, my knees are shaking. I'm sure all of my teammates' muscles are quivering too.

The weight on my back is heavy, as if an entire football team has landed on top of me, and it doesn't appear the other guys are going to fall off anytime soon. But I refuse to let my legs buckle beneath the team's combined weight.

Someone hollers out that we've got one more person to jump on top of us, and when he does, I think our team is going to break. Out of the corner of my eye, I spy one kid above, and as luck would have it, he loses his grip, topples off us, and falls to the ground.

All of my teammates cheer aloud the second everyone gets off our backs. Some high-five, and others jump on the losers, excited we didn't fail. The last half of the game is the craziest, and we call it Asses Up, which isn't a good thing for the losing team. They have to line up and bend over while holding their ankles as each one of the winners takes a turn whipping each loser. Usually a leather belt is used, or we wind up hitting them in the ass with a four-inch rubber handball. We use whatever is on hand, but it's brutal to receive a lashing from a leather belt no matter how much muscle is behind it.

There was always some sort of violence involved no matter what game we wound up playing. No one escaped from Johnny on the Pony by going home bruise-free. All of us wound up with marks and bruises all over us, and there'd always be that one who got a black eye. There were the rare occasions, however, when the mass number of people would fall on top of someone in such a way that they'd wind up with a broken limb.

Nobody has mercy in any of these games either. Even our closest of friends are still aggressive toward each other. Despite the games being this rough, the majority of us are tough enough that nobody ever goes home crying. We'd play different games and run hard like this all day long throughout the summer months, and by the day's end, we'd all be thick with dirt and sweat from just being boys.

The majority of the other kids go back home midday, leaving only a handful of us boys in the schoolyard. We decide to relax in the shade under one of the bigger trees and play some cards and dice. And I swear, we're not ten minutes into the game when suddenly, we see this guy in his late teens running right past us, panic-stricken.

We all stop playing out of sheer curiosity, wanting to see what the heck is going on with this guy, because either he's strung out on drugs, or he's running for his life.

We follow the guy's movements and watch him sprint across the length of the school as a large car sits on the opposite end of the building and revs its engine, making its presence known.

There are only three different places you can come into the schoolyard from, and judging by how many cars I see, they've got all exits covered. Another car comes in from behind the runner, driving over the grass, weaving around the potholes, and rapidly gaining on him. The guy glances over his shoulder and tries to run even faster, but there is no outrunning a vehicle.

He's out of breath, but I have to give the guy credit. He doesn't slow down, especially when he sees a big black Lincoln entering the grounds, and it's heading straight for him. It's coming in at Mach speed, kicking up dust behind its wheels.

He quickly turns back around, changing direction, and starts off in a renewed sprint heading toward the fence line. I think he's going to try to hop the fence in one leap, but then he realizes there is another black car with tinted windows idling on the other side of the fence, which happens to be on the end of my block.

It's as if whoever is after him has already anticipated his every move. He has nowhere to go; he's trapped. The cars begin closing in on him from all sides.

A couple men jump out of their car and hop the fence at the end of my block, and before the poor guy knows it, he's being surrounded by at least a half-dozen men carrying baseball bats.

Panicked, he holds out hands as if to stop them, but it does no good. Too many men are advancing on him, and when they corner him, they're not even interested in what he has to say. They waste no time jumping into action, and all I see is one big blur of several wooden bats being wielded back and forth and possessing enormous striking power.

The runner is absolutely helpless against the onslaught. He cries out, begging for mercy, but his pleas to gain some leniency go ignored. The guys are too absorbed with wanting to achieve an end result.

Blood curling screams fill the air just before he falls to his knees. He's now at the perfect height for these men to get some really good hits to his head, and that is exactly what happens. The sound of a wooden bat cracking against a skull is so loud I think it's the bat that has splintered, but it's not. His head is split open, and all my friends and I can do is watch as he keels over, falling flat on the ground, rolling around in indescribable pain.

With his head split half open, blood is spurting everywhere. He's getting a beating beyond recognition, right in front of us kids.

One particular man, who's not getting his hands

dirty, stares at us for a brief moment before he saunters toward us, looking very relaxed despite what's going on around him. He takes a long drag of his cigarette, lifts his chin to blow out the smoke over his left shoulder. He's a smooth operator—a mobster, actually. His Italian characteristics, neatly pressed dress pants, and the fedora he's wearing give him away. I could've easily stereotyped him as one, but I don't need those clues to know exactly who he is.

I'm constantly surrounded by mob affiliations, and many of them are personal friends of my father and uncle, knowing them through all their gambling connections and card games. I've been raised to be street-smart, very observant, and I understand the way things work around here.

I can also tell he's the one in charge of these men, the ones who are doing his dirty work. His thumb and forefinger pinch the butt of his cigarette as he brings the edge of it to his lips, taking in another deep pull of nicotine. I watch him closely, making sure he keeps his distance from me and my friends.

With a quick lift of his chin, he speaks in a gruff voice, "Hey, kids." He exhales another long stream of white smoke, adding, "How's everything going?"

"Fine," I answer, speaking for everyone in my group. I shrug as if he is boring me. I'm only left to assume the guy getting beaten owes this one money or has crossed him in some way.

The men continue to wail on this now crippled up

man as we all sit here and watch with passive interest. The shrill cries that previously filled the air have subsided, and taking their place are small, helpless whimpers, which are becoming less frequent too.

The life slowly drains out of him, and I figure he's about to pass out or die—whichever one happens to come first.

"Just don't worry about it," the mobster says with an air of authority. It sounds as if he's trying to keep us calm, or prevent us from freaking out over the barbaric scene, which is quite laughable. As kids, one would think all my friends and I would get up screaming and yelling the second all those big guys unfolded from their cars with their baseball bats. But in all truthfulness, none of us are the least bit concerned about what's taking place. It's too common a scene, and sadly, these regular occurrences now meant nothing to us.

"Yeah—whatever," I reply nonchalantly in my deep, froggy voice. This was so every day that these guys aren't even concerned they could be identified, and that's because they knew they wouldn't be.

I glance over and see the battered man has finally given up the fight. His T-shirt is soaked with his own fluids as his body lies lifeless in a pool of his own blood. The men finally stop their attacking as they stand in a circle surrounding the unmoving victim, breathing heavily from their workout. Each and every baseball bat is stained a deep red.

"Not gonna have any issues, are we?" he asks, just to make sure we're all on the same page.

I tilt my head to the side as I scrutinize this nicely dressed man. I make sure to hold his gaze, and as I do, I tell him in a serious, even tone, "Not a problem here." He nods his head in satisfaction, and then flicks his cigarette off into the distance as if his job is now done, making sure us kids aren't going to be a problem for him.

The police sirens sound off in the distance, and the instant they do, the men quickly get back in their cars and leave the vicinity as fast as they came barreling in. I guess one of the neighbors had called the police.

Joey nudges me to get my attention. I turn around and realize he's already dealing out cards. Everybody gets back to their own business, so I grab my five cards to see what I've got.

There must be about six cop cars that come plowing through the schoolyard with their white and blue lights flashing and their loud sirens blaring. Not too long after, an ambulance shows up, and after the paramedics start IVs and stabilize him, they carefully load the guy onto a stretcher to get him into the ambulance.

In the interim, one of the officers steps over to our little circle, and asks in disbelief, "Why in the hell are you all just sitting there?" He scans over each one of us, wide-eyed and in shock, full of disbelief that all of us have been so complacent.

I take in his overall appearance, from his short, salt-and-pepper hair, crisp blue uniform, and shiny black shoes, as the look on my face gives off my own expression of incredulity. He can't be serious. I mean—I have no idea what this cop was thinking... that a bunch of little kids like us could've gone up against a handful of mobsters who were swinging baseball bats? Or what if we would've run off to get the guy help? That would not have gone over well with them either. It's not how the streets work. It's about minding your own business, and you might make it to live another day. The motto on the streets was: if it didn't concern you personally, it was none of your business.

By the day's end, it seems as if everyone has already forgotten about the baseball bat incident. All of us hear mothers' voices coming from all over the neighborhood, shouting out from the back of their kitchen windows, "It's dinnertime!"

With all of us playing outside all day, we're all exhausted and hungry. So we begin to break up and head home. It's funny, though, hearing all the mothers shouting out for their kids to come home. It's like a chorus on steroids and off-key, but it's music to my ears, because I'm starved.

As my friends and I make our way back home, we cut through people's yards, everyone having hung out their clothes to dry on clotheslines. Every backyard is a mismatch of quilted colors hanging out for the world to see, and some can't help but make fun of each other's laundry.

"Hey, Johnny." Charlie asks, "How do you catch a bra?" I shrug, knowing he's going to have a corny joke, so I don't answer him. "You set up a boobie trap," he cackles out with laughter.

"You're so stupid," I tell him jokingly.

A few guys chuckle around me as Joey pipes in. He points to a woman's bra hanging out to dry on the clothesline. "That's a double D. You know what that stands for?"

We all shake our heads, as he answers, "Double damn." We all burst out with laughter.

"You wish you could handle what came with that bra," Charlie retorts. "You'd injure yourself trying to get that one off."

"Shut the hell up, man. That's my momma's," someone says defensively from behind us.

"Well, damn," Joey states in excitement, turning around to face the kid. "Get us a couple, will ya? We could make double barrel sling shots with 'em!"

Chapter 8

The train station runs above ground only two blocks away from my home near Jamaica Avenue. The J train extends through all the areas of Brooklyn, going into Manhattan, as well as stopping through every bad neighborhood in between. My friends and I usually take the L route, which goes through Queens in order to get us into Manhattan.

It wasn't a big deal to ride these train routes by myself. I was well primed for the streets by age five, so I rode the trains in order to get to the subways within the city all by myself. Public transportation was a breeze, and despicable as it was, the adults on these trains would try to con me, but they couldn't—no one could. I was too wise for my age, and I understood from the get-go how this world worked. Plus, I was being raised to not be afraid of anything. My education didn't take place in school as much as it did on the streets, and I was learning the streets at an alarming rate.

Sometimes we'd ride this train by jumping onto the back end where the chains were, and we'd ride it until the next stop, all the while hanging on for dear life. We lived for the thrill. Things changed when a friend of mine found a way to beat the system. It was the most genius way to get into the city and ride the subways for free. He was an older kid who was able to bend the metal turnstile at our station by standing on it with the force of his weight. Then he'd bounce up and down on the apparatus until he could curve it enough so all of us kids could slip through the narrow passageway. Since I was so little, it was easy for me to pass through.

It's the regular group of friends I have with me today—Kevin, Joey, Charlie, Jerry, and my brother. Our destination is Times Square, which is the most popular area for all kinds of debauchery to take place. It's the inner city's refuge for prostitution, peepshows, crime, and drugs.

We take all the memorized routes on the subways, enjoying being able to goof off. It's close to the holidays, so things are busier than normal. People are bundled up in winter jackets, scarves, and knitted hats. I rub my hands together, trying to create some friction for warmth, and then I cup my hands together to breathe some warm air on them.

The subways are just as infested with graffiti as the underground concrete walls of each subway stop. It's full of wall-to-wall art, housing a myriad of colors, hidden messages, and full of individual expression. The brightly colored spray paints used have now lost their vibrancy as years of dirt and grime have clung to the walls, creating a dismal film. I suppose the bleakness is poetic for the times we're living in.

The subway train screeches loudly as it comes to our stop. The doors slide open and we slowly make our way off the train, the majority of travelers getting off at our stop as well. The stench among the heavy crowds is full of body odor, cigarettes, grease, and grime. We push our way through the sea of people, each one trying to shove their way toward the exit.

As we shuffle along, getting closer to the stairs, I notice a big, tough, black guy standing beside the steps with his back against the wall. He's got a brown beanie on his head, and a very dirty, worn-out, red plaid flannel jacket, but what makes me take pause is the expression on his face. He's the size of two linebackers, and he looks angry.

I hear his voice above the crowd, as he threatens in a powerful and menacing tone, "Give me a dollar." He's not asking; with a heated glare, he's demanding it from a passerby, and by the looks of it, I don't think the other man is going to give in.

Usually, I come across the everyday hustlers who approach people for a token or thirty cents spouting the usual, "I forgot my change. Can you help me out?" Or sometimes it's the guitar players and subway musicians decked out in their hippy clothes adorned with beads and fringes, hoping passersby will drop their loose change in their empty instrument cases. Lower on the social scale and the most common, however, are the alcoholics, cripples, and unshaven bums dressed in rags. Oddly, they're the most physically and mentally ill, yet the most harmless.

Beggars and hustlers are spread far and wide from one edge of the city to the other. Some are cunning and others mild, but they're all like a flock of hungry pigeons and exist in out-of-control numbers.

But this guy here… he's being a bully beggar. His pitch is coming off as a real threat. My brows furrow as I think something is really off about him. I keep my eye on him as we get closer, but in a blur of movement, this two-hundred-forty-something-pound man suddenly goes berserk. He pulls out what must be a five-inch-long knife then steps forward to plunge his blade into the gut of the man who refused to give him money. The man drops to his knees in agonizing pain, clutching his stomach with a fierce grip as blood starts to ooze from between his fingertips.

If no one was paying attention to what was about to go down, they are now. The offender is immediately given a wide berth as people begin to scatter and the women scream. Some innocent bystander pulls the injured man out of harm's way, but that doesn't stop this nut from jabbing his knife in the air toward the others who are trying to escape up the stairs.

My friends and I back up a few steps to avoid getting trampled. This psycho has got to be on drugs. Some people jump back on the subway; others are just trying to wait this guy out. People are shouting and screaming in another wave of panic as he lunges forward again, attempting to slash two young boys who are off to the side. Thank God they were quick and able to duck and dodge the monster.

With what seems like forever to get him subdued, which is really only a few minutes, a handful of cops rush in to hold him at gunpoint. Once they have him in handcuffs and escort him out of the subway, most everyone is shaken up and terror stricken. Most everyone but me.

As I stand here, all I can't think about is how angry I'm getting over this situation. I glance at my brother, thinking that, in spite of our young age, together we have what it takes to run up the steps and take out that beast. As if he can already read my mind, he shakes his head. I despise being part of a victimized crowd, and I know I'd hate it worse if I were singled out to be someone's prey. I grit my teeth, hating the feeling of helplessness.

I absorbed today's lesson with sobering clarity. I swear to be better prepared to protect myself from now on. With the times I'm living in, it's been proven time and again that no one is going to step in to help anyone in their time of need. There is no knight in shining armor, no Superman to the rescue, nothing. I'm only so big, and my hands can only take me so far in a fight. I only have myself to rely on, and I've been caught off guard one too many times without a decent weapon on hand. It's time to take more extreme measures.

If someone wants to pull a knife on me, I need to pull out a bigger one, and if someone wants to point a gun in my face, I need to have my own. The fact I'm not even twelve yet is no longer an issue. It's time for me to turn the tides and take things to the next level. I will not only match these guys weapon for weapon, but I will do one better; I'll beat them to the punch.

Joey breaks the ice after a few minutes, and says, "Well, that was exciting." All of us glance his way. He shrugs. "What? It was exciting." I shake my head at him, and that quick, the harrowing moment is put behind us and we're off again, with our own mission of exploration getting back underway.

We hit the stairs and ascend toward the outside world of the busy city streets, each of us taking two steps at a time. The noise from above reverberates downward and through the stairwell as hundreds of cars honk their horns, sounding like a symphony of drunk trumpet players. I've lived here so long I don't even smell the exhaust fumes from the cars anymore.

A burst of frigid air nips at the tips of my ears the second we step out of the stairwell and into the cold near Times Square. A massive shiver rolls through me.

This is the kind of cold that goes straight through one's bones, but we all tough it out.

We pass a score of homeless men who are huddling over a large grate in the sidewalk to catch the warm, humid air as it escapes from below. Once winter sets in, and the temperatures drop to an ungodly low, if they stay over these grates to keep warm through the night, it will become a death sentence for most.

This area was once full of upscale hotels and theaters, but all I've ever known Times Square to be is a refuge for the unwanted.

We pass by a newsstand in the middle of the sidewalk, the daily newspapers lined up in such a way one can't help but catch the headline: **Ford said: "Drop dead—and give zero bailout to the city."**

It goes ignored by many passersby, including myself. There's no way I comprehend the full implications of that statement at my age, but it's the article below the Ford one that I read with understanding. **"Times Square: the crime hub of the city. Over 2,300 crimes committed every year within a one-block radius."**

As we walk farther down the street, we approach a few punks who are playing hip-hop music on their stereo speakers as they sit on a set of stairs. When we pass them, they give us a curt nod. We return the gesture, acknowledge them, and keep moving. I suppose if one were looking from the outside in, me and my group appear just as rough and rugged as the next group of kids on the streets. Everybody trying to be tough and powerful to avoid being a victim.

New York stops for nothing. This city stays busy twenty-four hours a day, and it's filled with people from all walks of life. There's trash splayed out all over the road and sidewalks, and the panorama of sleazy strip clubs, bars, and hotels that rent out by the hour are the city's main existence. The entire metropolis has this dingy-gray appearance, most likely from years of pollution, and it clings to the streets and buildings as if it were bonded with glue.

The hustle and bustle is so condensed on the sidewalks it makes me wonder if people even work for a living. Bright lights, blinking colors of all kinds, come at us from all angles. Neon signs flashing 25-cents for peepshows are in every other storefront window we walk by.

A prostitute slips out from the back seat of a big black Cadillac as it idles curbside in front of a hotel. She's wearing a scowl as she cuts in front of us, making a beeline for the hotel's entrance. A few of us trip over our feet to keep from bumping into her, but it's when a large man bolts out of the car right on her heels that forces us to come to a complete stop. He reaches out and grabs at her bare arm to pull her back into him, and he doesn't look happy either.

The woman's mascara is a mess, the black color running underneath her eyes, making her look like a raccoon. She lets out a blood-curdling scream while trying to yank her arm from his tight grasp, but then she's silenced with a resounding slap to her face. I'm taken aback initially, but then something inside me winds up, turning into a rage I haven't felt before. I don't like seeing a woman being treated like this, and God help me, I want to help her. I scan over her clothing, realizing she hardly has any on. It's freezing cold outside. The man has a high-end coat on, while the woman is only wearing a short, tight mini skirt with black, shiny boots that go past her knees, and a skimpy top with spaghetti straps to reveal her cleavage.

Joey grabs me by the arm, pulling me off to the side of the couple, which forces me to skirt around the scene. I twist my head around as we're leaving to get a good look at the pimp. There's no doubt in my mind what he is. He has on the classic hat and the long colorful jacket, all while sporting his big Cadillac.

"Forget about it," Joey urges. "Come on." He gives me another tug to pull me along and away from their argument. Another block away, and I'm accosted by brightly lit neon signs flashing everywhere. One of the signs is a pink silhouette, depicting the shapely figure of a mature woman's body with the infamous 25-cents sign advertised beneath with flickering lights. These peepshows are lined up one after the other all along the city's streets, each one trying to tempt passersby inside.

I don't know if there's a sign stating one had to be of legal age or not, but nobody stops our underage group from entering these shows. We wouldn't have paid attention to them anyway. We're just a bunch of mischievous kids, passing the time as we test and push our boundaries and limits, just to see how far we can take things.

Jerry gives me a push from behind, steering me to the right. Before I know it, the six of us are cramming ourselves into a small cubicle.

"What the hell?" I blurt out, perplexed and taken off guard, because I'd never done this before.

"Hang on," Jerry assures me with a devious grin. "You gotta watch this."

Someone shuts the door behind us as we all stand shoulder-to-shoulder and very squished. These rooms are only made to hold one person, not a group. There's only one stool in the room, and who's standing the farthest from the front climbs onto it so he can see above everyone else's heads. The booth itself is dark and dirty with old red paint peeling off the walls, but I guess, in the scheme of things, nobody really gives a flip what the booth looks like, given the fact something alluring and sinful is about to go down.

I watch as Jerry drops a quarter into a narrow slot next to the red tapestry curtain, and then we all stand in silence, waiting in anticipation. Excitement is in the air. I can sense it rolling off the other guys from behind me. Music begins to play from a sound system overhead, and then the lights go off. It's now pitch black, except for a bright light filtering in from the edges of the curtain.

As the fabric shade begins to rise, so do the adrenaline levels in the tight confines of our small space. I guess this is considered to be an adult version of an arcade, but this game is full of cheap and illicit thrills, not the pinball machines making loud noises when scoring points.

The first thing I see as the curtain lifts are tanned and very muscled calves and red glitter high heels. Inch by inch, long, sexy legs are revealed to us while all the guys let out low groans. Once this tempting female on her little stage is fully on display, she swings her hips to the sultry music playing above.

Hot pants and crop tops are prevalent among the streets, but that's not what's on display here. The woman's entire body is wrapped in skin-tight slender strips of sequined pink fabric, creating a lattice pattern with each crossing of the material. The design does nothing to hide anything—it's all for show—accentuating her every curve from head to toe with strategically placed metal studs. The bling shimmers and sparkles from the overhead lighting, which draws my attention to her barely covered body parts. Long, blonde locks of thick curled hair cascade down her backside, and it sways with her as she dances.

My jaw drops open while excitement races

through me, as this is probably every little boy's wet dream—to see a sexy Marilyn Monroe type of woman provocatively showing off her wide, sexy hips with a large rack that men would give a week's pay to have the privilege of touching. A blinking light below the coin depository catches my eye. I give Jerry a nudge, but it looks as if he's already aware of our time running out. I watch as he scrambles to dig into his front pocket for another coin to keep the curtain from closing. Nobody wants the show to end—not now, when things are just getting good.

~~*

All of this porn within the city, ranging from hardcore to softcore and everything in between. It was ran by a man who was referred to as the King of Porn. His real name was Robert DiBernardo, also known as DB, which at the time meant absolutely nothing to me. I had no idea who he was or that the city and all their streets were ran by the mafia. I had even less of a clue that, one day, I would be in charge of administering an infinite amount of violence on behalf of the Gambino Crime Family. I was living on a fast track with a ticket straight to hell and didn't even know it.

Chapter 9

Waking at first light, my arms slip out of the warmth of my covers as I stretch my arms wide and give a big yawn. I rub the sleep from my eyes then suddenly remember what today is. Within a second, I'm wide awake and peeling away my blanket. The winter's temperature has infiltrated the warmth of the room overnight, leaving a chill in the morning air. I set my feet on the cold wooden floor and a shiver rolls right through me, which goes ignored, all because of the delicious aroma that has drifted into my room. I inhale deeply and close my eyes, wearing a grin. It's my grandmother's famous french toast, and it happens to be my all-time favorite breakfast food.

I glance over at my brother who's still sleeping and decide not to wake him yet. My gaze sweeps over the room as I take in all the shapely women plastered on all four of the walls in our bedroom. My brother and I have decorated our bedroom with Dallas Cowboys

Cheerleader posters as if it were wallpaper. The women are so popular I'd overhear many girls in our school talking with excitement how they dream of one day becoming part of the famous cheerleaders.

We have at least a dozen different posters of them decked out in their full Dallas Cowboys uniforms. Each poster is in large, full-color print, with the women modeling in varying poses. Their signature white boots gleam on every poster tacked to the wall, but my favorite part of their uniform is all the small white short-shorts they wear along with a wide belt wreathed in blue stars. To top it off, they bore cleavage from their tight blue bikini-style tops, complemented by a white-and-blue-starred vest. Every single woman on the cheer team is stunning, breathtaking in their own way.

During live football games, the cameras would occasionally focus on these women as they danced a routine, and then again for the full show they'd put on at halftime. My eyes were always locked on the TV screen for this show, every bit as much as the game itself. Their tiny outfits always bared an abundance of toned muscles and unblemished feminine skin, yet they were still covered enough to leave a little mystery to the imagination.

I slip out of the bedroom as quietly as possible, and then head downstairs to my grandparents' floor as I follow my nose. The fresh smell of my grandmother's cooking already has my stomach growling. I enter the kitchen to be greeted by a warm smile. "Johnny *kapitane*," my grandmother says in Albanian, her voice full of affection.

"Mornin', Grandma." I return her smile as she runs her fingers through my mussed-up hair. Although she's only five feet tall and a tad stocky, she's the matriarch of our family. She would always wear flower dresses like Aunt Bee from the *Andy Griffith Show*, and when she cooked, she kept an apron tied around her. My stomach grumbles again and she lets me go, setting off to fill a plate full of french toast for me.

"Eat up, *spirti*," she singsongs. "Today is a special day."

"Yes!" I respond excitedly, pouring maple syrup all over my plate. "Dallas Cowboys and Miami Dolphins," I tell her, as if she doesn't already know. She grins at me over her shoulder.

There's a charge of excitement in the air, and in early anticipation of the game, I'm already wearing my Cowboy slippers and sweatshirt, which sports their big blue insignia on the front. I have more Dallas Cowboys paraphernalia, but I'll grab those closer to game time.

"Mmm…" I hum the second the warm bread and all its flavor hits my tongue. "This is the best, Grandma," I tell her, my voice full of enthusiasm. She laughs at me as she stands over the stovetop and the most amazing smell from her cooking permeates the walls of the entire household.

Our house will be full of nonstop activity later today, along with endless male banter for the Super Bowl VI game. I can hardly contain myself. First, the Dallas Cowboys have made it to the Super Bowl, and second, it's our family's all-time favorite team. My uncle, Sam, who lives on the very top floor of our house, is actually friends with Mike Ditka.

Albanian music plays softly in the background, something my grandmother enjoys listening to every day. I savor every single bite, stuffing myself full.

My grandfather walks into the kitchen with his newspaper under his arm as I'm dredging the last piece of bread through the lake of syrup on my plate. "Johnny *kapitane!*" he greets me with enthusiasm, as he sits down beside me with a wide smile. All of our family calls him Dati, but his American name is Jimmy. He acquired this nickname early on, because as kids, we couldn't pronounce his name, so the endearment stuck.

I always made time to sit down with my grandfather, especially when he ate breakfast, but sometimes during the school week, I'm unable to. I watch him with interest as he removes the newspaper from under his arm and then proceeds to spread it out on the tabletop. He orders the Albanian newspaper, which gets delivered to the house daily, because he enjoys reading the news from back home.

I look up to him with full-on admiration, and I

hate he's getting older. I take notice of his receding hairline and all the gray in his hair, no longer having any of the once vibrant black hair that was so predominant at one time. He's so intellectual and distinguished, and just like my father, he wasn't school-educated, but he was self-taught. He had the uncanny ability to learn on his own, having taught himself to speak six different languages. Besides the obvious Albanian language, he learned English, Greek, Italian, German, and Turkish.

He must feel me staring up at him, because he pauses from reading the paper, dipping his chin down as he looks at me over the top rim of his glasses.

"You okay, Johnny?" he asks.

I nod, and as I do, I can see something flash across his eyes before he cocks his head to the side, giving me a grin. He lays the newspaper off to the side on the table to give me his full attention at the same time my grandmother places a stack of french toast in front of him. The breakfast goes ignored as he shifts in his chair to face me.

Dati wraps his arm around my shoulders and brings me in for a side hug, squeezing me tight. I'm not sure I could ever compare the two heroes in my life, my father and grandfather. It's impossible. The two men are the absolute cornerstone of my world, and I love them both equally. Yet one couldn't be more different than the other. It's as if each man was born from opposite ends of the spectrum.

Unlike my father, Dati never gambled, and he never got himself a tattoo. He was an old-style guy who, no matter what, was the family provider. He was the most unselfish human being I'd ever met, and he looked after everyone in his household and then some. *Everybody* loves him, but I'd like to think no one loves him more than me. If my grandfather had to work a hundred hours a week to take care of our family, he'd do it without complaint. That's how committed to us he is.

My grandfather and dad might have their own tempers and fits of rage occasionally, but aside from that, they are both very loving and caring men, always having an overabundance of deep affection and compassion for us.

Dati lets me go, and orders, "Let me see your muscle." As he says this, he chuckles out loud, because he always jokes and laughs with me. I'm constantly working out, yet I'm still a very skinny kid.

I roll up the thick material of my Cowboys sweatshirt and bend my arm at the elbow, proudly flexing my bicep for him.

He places his two fingers over my scrawny arm muscle then lets out a loud whistle. "Whoa!" he exclaims with a mixed amount of pride and awe. "You're stronger than a whistle. Wow!"

I beam with pride. Dati is always building me up, and his words only encourage me to work out harder and grow bigger.

"Johnny is skinny—but strong," he tells me proudly, speaking in that special Albanian accent of his. "I like that you're tough."

"Thanks," I reply.

He pauses, his expression turning serious. "Your daddy—Meti—he'll teach you to fight. Meti teaches everybody how to fight." I nod in agreement, hanging on his every word. "I like... nobody can bully you."

My grandfather was the only one with whom I have this unspeakable bond with. Nobody else in our family could claim this kindred type of relationship with him but me. These one-on-one talks are always reserved for me.

"Johnny—you Albanian," he proudly says in broken English, as he points to the Albanian flag hanging on the kitchen wall. Bright red material shimmers against the light coming off the stained-glass chandelier, and in the center of the flag is a silhouette of a black double-headed eagle. My grandfather schooled me numerous times about the meaning of our flag, making sure I understood the red color stood for bravery, strength, and valor, while the double-headed eagle represented the sovereign state of Albania. My grandmother even has cherished knickknacks from their homeland spread all over their apartment floor, along with old family photographs hanging in frames. No matter what peril the country fell into by the hands of politics, they were always proud to be Albanian.

Dati hugs me again as he tells me he loves me, adding, "You got to be smart, you got to work, make money, and have a good life. I came here—and I work and I work." He gestures with his hand, telling me, "We have good house. Everybody is together. You got to be like me—take care of everybody."

He looks into my eyes, making sure I understand what it is he's trying to convey. For some reason, he always chose me to have this talk with, which leads me to believe he must see something inside of me. As if I have a special part of his DNA that values the unity of family and he's relying on me to one day pick up the slack when he might no longer be able to.

My grandfather never cared for gambling; in fact, he hated it. He saw the effects it had on our entire family. He was constantly unloading on my dad and uncles, yelling at them when we were all gathered around the dinner table on the weekends. It was pretty much a weekly lecture he'd give them while he had them all in one place, not caring who was at the table. He called them all lazy, tried to shame and humiliate them for spending all their money on lost causes. It would upset him to no end that the men of our household weren't sacrificing and working hard to bring in a steady income to contribute to everyone's betterment.

"All right?" he asks.

"Yeah," I respond with a smile.

"Yeah?" he repeats my answer.

I nod. "Yeah, Grandpa."

With that confirmation, he says, "Atta boy, Johnny." Then he pats my thigh, indicating our little conversation is over. He turns to his cooling breakfast and cuts through his French toast to take a bite. He eats in silence for a few minutes as he peruses the paper, and then after he swallows another mouthful, he looks at me for a moment with pride gleaming in his eyes. "Johnny, go lay down on the couch," he tells me, lifting his chin toward the living room.

I grin, because my grandfather knows I love to have my back rubbed. He always treats me like a king, making me feel special at every turn, and after special talks such as these, he then has my grandmother rub my back—which is just short of heaven.

~~*

It would only take a little over ten years for me to relieve my grandfather of his family duties. I would've never imagined the possibilities I had at my age, but I was driven to the extremes. When I wanted something, I went after it with almost superhuman powers, not allowing anything to get in the way of my goals.

Providing for my family the way my grandfather did came at a price, and I'm not referring to what it cost me both mentally and physically—but in the generosity I gave to the others. I did nobody any favors by enabling certain family members to become dependent on me. It made some helpless, needy, and incapable of self-sustainment, which would come back to haunt me on so many levels.

Chapter 10

Our house was never lonely, never quiet, and always full of activity, and even though there's always fighting and screaming going on, there's always action in equal measure. Today of all days is even more intense. It's been nothing but excitement and pure adrenaline rushes since noon today.

It's all about football, gambling, pizza, soda, snacks, and the most dynamic part of all, is the camaraderie of all us guys having gathered under one roof. The combined energy of our convening together gives rise to a high-energy and nonstop environment. Makes me feel as if I belong to something significant, almost like a boys club, but better, because what exists here is a genuine solidarity of unity, loyalty, and a steadfast brotherhood. From my family, extended family, friends, and neighbors, we've all come together to enjoy the fun and games.

"Freddy said Miami is five!" my dad shouts out as

he stands inches outside our front door, projecting his voice up the set of stairs that lead to the next level of our house.

"Well, I've got it six," my uncle, Sam, hollers back from the top of his landing, as he also stands outside his door.

As if watching a live tennis match, my father's neck turns from the right then to the left before he yells down the steps, this time to my uncle, Freddy. "Well, I got it at three!"

"Well, take it at three," Freddy shouts up to my dad, and with that news, my father again turns his head the other way to let Uncle Sam know the plan.

Every floor of our house has their own separate phone line, and they're mostly used for gambling. Each phone has these ten-foot-long coiled cords, and each one lost their buoyancy and spring a long time ago, exactly because of this type of scenario. With each man on their own floor, my dad and uncles would get as far into the hallway as they possibly could while they shouted up and down the stairs at each other. Each talking to different bookmakers at the same time while trying to compare notes and relay messages.

For me, witnessing these moments were some of the most comical events that took place throughout our house every game day.

Much planning went into these gambling ventures, and many times, a lot of money was at stake. Before anybody would bet on any sports game, my dad and uncles would always collaborate on an agreed upon game plan. They could always be found hovering over spreadsheets, each man squabbling and debating over different strategies and theories as to how much money to wager and how to allocate the funds. The second they finished devising their plans, all the men split up like pool balls on break, each going in different directions to call their own set of bookmakers.

I was taught, when betting on sports games, to pay attention to the points with extra scrutiny, because if they're off even a point or one-and-a-half points, it can be a big deal and a ton of money lost. We comb through many bookmakers in order to find the soft ones. This is so we can get an edge on the line. Getting this edge is supposed to help with the odds while betting with the hard bookmakers. We'd bet the same amount of money for both the hard and soft. An example would be a five-thousand bet to each set of bookmakers so we could catch the middle. I learned these terminologies, and all the ins and outs of gambling was a breeze for me to pick up on. It was never a foreign concept to me. I always caught on— and sometimes understood things too much.

All the adrenaline-infused minutes with the men shouting up and down the stairs as they all tried to collaborate as to who had what deal and with what point spread was highly entertaining.

Depending on which bookmakers had the better lines, and what each bookie was offering, it would be contingent as to the amount of money the men would put down. Hence the last minute shouting through the stairwell while on the phone, so everyone could be on the same page and agree.

"Shit, phone's busy," my dad utters under his breath as he tries to redial the same bookie's phone number for the second time. "Come on... come on." His voice is full of urgency. He looks down at his watch, because he's pressed for time and trying to get his bet in before the bookmaker quits taking calls for the game he's betting on.

"I feel like I'm dialing forever," he complains, agitated. "These phones are gonna turn off any minute now, and I've got only seconds to get through!" My dad's fingers frantically slip into the hole of the rotary dial. Number by number, he whips the rotary wheel around with such force I think he will rip the wheel off the base of the phone.

The bookmaker phones shut down for bets ten minutes before a game, and when the phones are turned off, they are cut off, and no one will take any more bets. "We've got four minutes before the phones close, so put that bet in now!" Uncle Freddy yells up the stairs.

"I'm trying to!" my dad shouts back with frustration. He's been dialing like crazy, over and over. His foot taps in anticipation as he dials the last digit, hoping this time he can talk to a bookie to place his bet.

From the top of the stairs, Uncle Sam yells down, "We've got Dallas plus six!"

My dad hollers up to my uncle with the phone receiver pressed tightly to his ear, "Bet five-thousand on that!"

I almost burst out with laughter. The hilarity and suspense of all the dynamics at play all at the same time is comical.

"Finally!" my dad exclaims, having reached the soft bookmaker he was after. He then places five thousand on the Miami Dolphins with a minus-three so he can catch what we call "the middle."

One team will obviously win, and the other lose, but if we win the middle, we'd walk away with ten grand just by betting this way.

If this was not the Super Bowl, and we were gambling during the season, my dad would go through this all over again at halftime with my uncles. All of them scheming as to what team they would bet on next to make up for any lost monies they might have encountered. We only have Sunday and Monday Night Football, so if they lost Sunday's bets, they'd try to make up for it on Monday, hoping to break even by playing the odds, while trying to make extra money.

At this point in my life, I already understand how all of this betting against the odds worked. I already know how to work with gambling ventures that hold higher odds, lower odds, and not only in the basic sense either, but in more complicated schemes.

~~*

Because my father loves to gamble—and I'm not talking just a little bit—he's obsessed with wanting to beat the odds. For him, it's about the thrill of winning, and being able to manipulate the players, all the while putting his money on the line.

He was damn good at gambling schemes too, but unfortunately, the winning streaks were always accompanied by losing streaks, and when he lost—well, everyone knew it. Since I grew up among a family of gamblers, it was easy to recognize the roller-coaster pattern of wins and losses. I knew the gambling mentality, and between my father and uncles, they taught me how to understand the odds. This knowledge also helped me be very streetwise. Because I was on the streets, and as I got older, and was making some of my own money I had put bets in for them using different bookmakers they were unaware of. My father and uncles were always coaching me, giving me an education in the things they were most proficient at, except nobody knew when to quit when they were ahead.

I watched firsthand the money coming in and going out, so it never really took me by surprise when, inevitably, someone would go broke. They would then need to borrow money so they could continue to gamble, thinking they'd be able to pull out of it. There were several times when my dad would ask us kids if we had a couple hundred bucks to spot him.

And that's how a gambler chases their money, a lesson I learned all before I hit the first grade. There's a sharp distinction between those who gamble and those who take the money as a bookie, and I picked up on it immediately.

A stark contrast, as different as black and white, and it was painfully obvious to me, but not to my father and uncles. This was because they were gamblers. Initially, I thought they loved the money, but it was the chase they loved more.

By watching them closely, it allowed me to make this differentiation, and it made me think. I knew that, by being a gambler, they'd never win, so I decided I didn't want to be the gambler. I wanted to be the guy taking the bets.

Chapter 11

There was this kid named George Deegan who stole the keys to PS 97, my elementary school. George had taken those keys to someone who would make spares, and gave me one of the copies. He was about six years older than me and my friends, and no longer went to my school. It became a collaborative effort, however, to conspire amongst one another to see what mischief we could get into by exploring the building at night. When it would turn dark, all of my friends and I would slip into the school building like a Navy Seal team on an undercover mission and infiltrate the inner sanctum of the elementary school.

We were a group of boys with idle time; most of the things we did were probably considered dangerous, but they weren't to us. We were always doing these stupid things just for the thrill of it. I suppose we never thought we'd get caught, that we were too smart, too conniving. Plus, we had the ability to keep these outings on the down-low, keeping secrets to ourselves.

The fact we were getting away with something we shouldn't be doing and having free reign of the school was an adrenaline rush. My idea of breaking into the school was to have a look around, cut loose, and play some games. Sometimes we'd have a game of basketball in the gym, and at other times, we'd bring girls with us and play games to get them to kiss us. Out of all the games we played inside the school, Ring-A-Leerio was everyone's favorite. There were endless dark recesses within the corridors and places within the classrooms to hide.

Of course, at some point, all good things must come to an end, and it wasn't too long afterward when this too much of a good thing had been infringed upon. George and a few of the older kids he was hanging out with had started to get brave. They began stealing school property such as TVs, expensive science and gym equipment.

Many of my friends in the fifth grade were good kids. They were the ones who weren't interested in belonging to a gang, especially at such a young age. They also didn't understand the streets the way I did, and they hadn't been exposed to the things I had seen. I was used to theft happening around me. Stealing was the way of the streets; it's all we knew, and it was what I was taught. We were poor, and everyone around me did what they had to do in order to survive.

Sadly, there were very few moral compasses to guide me from kindergarten on up, especially when my uncles, brother, and older friends continually coerced me into doing their bidding, and I didn't know any better. I'd get talked into shoplifting items, or they'd dare me to do something that always held an edge of adrenaline to it. They knew I'd rise to any challenge they put before me, because I loved being bold, daring, and fearless.

As a young kid I had been so brazen as to buy a pack of gum at the cash register, all the while having my pockets full of toys or whatever else I could get my hands on to steal. I even robbed illegal fireworks from someone's garage with a group of guys from the street, and then we turned around and sold them for a decent profit.

The way my father was raising me, driving and pushing me to be a fearless fighter, I wound up applying it to all aspects of my life. So the name of the game on the street was learning how to hustle, and if I had to live in and among these people, I had to be slicker and more cunning than they were.

Looking back now, I can see where my dad had sent me mixed messages. In one breath, he'd brag about me to anyone who'd listen to him. He was so full of pride that I was wild, and tough, even ballsy, but then he'd get upset when I got out of control.

So when George stole things with his older friends, that's when all the trouble started. The teachers began to notice things disappearing.

"Johnny Alite."

My head snaps up from my friend's desk then I turn around to face the front of the classroom, thinking I'm in trouble. When I make eye contact with my English teacher, her one eyebrow raises as if I'm already guilty of something. She tilts her head to the left, indirectly pointing at the man standing beside her.

Confused, I lean around the person sitting in front of me, stretching my neck to have a better look for myself. A clean-cut man dressed in dark slacks and a jacket stands with his arms crossed with an aura of authority about him. He doesn't look overbearing or threatening, but I'm thinking this doesn't bode well for me.

"Johnny," my teacher says, "this gentleman would like to have a word with you." The man leans in to whisper something in my teacher's ear. When he's done, she clears her throat, adding, "Please go outside in the hallway."

The classroom is so quiet I could hear a pin drop. I stand up then make my way to the front of the room, and as I do, I feel everyone's eyes burning into my backside. I'm not sure what this is about, but I maintain a poker face. Something I'm very good at doing no matter the odds.

As I approach, the man walks with me toward the door then ushers me out into the hallway. When the classroom door closes behind us, I'm met with two other men. They're both dressed the same as the first man. One guy is short and stout, and he reaches into the inner breast pocket of his jacket, producing an official-looking badge.

"Johnny," he says as he puts his badge away, "I'm Detective Smith, and these two men are Detectives Spinelli and Woodham."

I keep my mouth shut during the introductions and cock my head to the side, wondering why they would want to speak with me.

"We have under good authority that you obtained a set of keys to this school," the detective half-accuses, looming over me. My guess is he's trying to create a threatening presence.

I don't miss a beat as I give the detective a blank stare, and deadpan, "I don't have any keys." I hold out my empty hands as if that should explain everything. "I don't know what you're talking about."

Even though this is my first official introduction to the police, I'm not intimidated in the least. All I can think about is the fact they don't have any evidence. There's no way they can prove anything.

"Are you sure 'bout that?" the other plain-clothed cop says from my left.

I lift my chin to stare up at this six-foot-tall and skinny man, repeating my words with conviction, "I don't have any keys. You got the wrong person." As I stand here, I'm thinking my problem is already solved.

I'll just throw my own set of copied keys George gave me in the junkyard next to my house so they can't find it. Nobody can.

The detective studies me for a brief moment in quiet conjecture, then adds, "Well, let's see what your mother has to say about this, shall we?"

I give a noncommittal shrug just before one of the men grasps my upper arm to escort me down to the principal's office. On my way to the office, I half wonder if they're trying to bluff me. Did they really call my mother in? My curiosity stops the second I enter a private office and see her sitting in a chair, worrying her hands like she's rubbing in lotion.

"I'll give you both a minute," one of the officers tells my mom, as I'm lead into the room. The door shuts, leaving both of us alone... then silence. I look around the small room lined with painted cinder blocks that has seen better days, making sure we are truly alone.

"Do you got keys to this school, Johnny?" my mom asks, sounding scared. I don't know why she's scared, but it irks me that these men have upset her.

"No, Ma," I tell her. I pause for a minute. The only thing on my mind at this point is whether or not my dad knows of this meeting. "You didn't tell Daddy about this, did you?" I ask, worried. "Cause he'll kick my ass." This was the one and only thing I did fear— my father.

"Then give them the keys, Johnny," my mom

pleads. "Your father's going to beat you!" she implores it in a way meant to scare me.

"I don't have any keys, Ma. I don't know why everyone's saying I do," I say forcefully, full of confidence. "I didn't do it. Somebody else did, but I'm not telling you who." My mother doesn't look happy about my lack of cooperation, but she's all too familiar with my obstinate personality. She shakes her head, knowing there's no sense in arguing with me. The conversation is over.

She gets up to open the door to let the three cops come back into the room. They're looking at my mother expectantly, as if she could be the one to reason with me.

Detective Smith comes to stand toe-to-toe with me and crosses his arms. He's going to try and pressure me. I can see the look in his eyes, but he has no effect on me whatsoever.

"Do you happen to know George Deegan?" he asks arrogantly.

"Yeah," I reply with a shrug.

"Well, he says you have a copy of the school keys."

"He's a liar," I spit out, almost interrupting the officer before he finished his sentence. I can't believe the jerk gave me up, saying I had the keys and then blamed it all on me. Despite this, I still won't give him up, or anyone else for that matter.

After going back and forth for a while, these men

finally understood my story wasn't going to change, and I held my ground. They had nothing, nor could they prove anything. I suppose it could have been George who told on me, but part of me believes it was also the other kids. The ones who didn't run within our circle but only hung out with us on occasion and never got in trouble. I suppose they broke very easily under the pressure, but the detectives had no way of knowing who was stealing stuff from the school property.

There were other keys; I wasn't the only one who had a copy. But the second I get home today, I'm throwing the evidence away at the abandoned house next to ours. It's full of tall, thick weeds, leaves, and debris, and will easily erase all proof. Nobody will ever find it, and nobody will ever know the truth.

Chapter 12

Without a cloud in the sky, the hot summer sun beams down on me from high above. I wipe the sweat from my brow with the back of my hand and glance at the thermometer hanging on one of the columns of my friend's back porch. We're in the midst of a rare heatwave. It's not even noon yet, and we're already climbing into the mid-nineties. Combine that with the humidity and it's sweltering.

During the summer months, if my friends and I aren't playing sports, heading into the city, or getting into trouble of some kind, we could all be found hanging out together at one particular house in our neighborhood. This house is our main hangout, our go-to place. The parents always have an open-door policy for their children's friends, and they're good about making one feel more than welcome.

Since our neighborhood is predominantly Irish, it goes without saying that this family is very active within the Catholic church. They were also big on large families, sometimes having up to ten children. Most of my friends go to the local private Catholic school, but since I don't, I wind up hanging out with them after school to play baseball. The summer months is when we get to spend the most time together.

Despite the fact I fell into the category of non-churchgoer, my Catholic friends nor their parents passed judgement on those who weren't Catholic. My family wasn't religious, and my grandparents, having come from Albania, never thought of religion as something important to focus on. Survival and escaping political oppression from the Albanian government were their main concerns, as well as trying to make a decent living within the States.

I've grown up with this family since I was five, and knowing them for well over seven years now, they've pretty much adopted me. I'm allowed to go to their house any time I want, and I take full advantage, especially the times when my father isn't around.

I only started going to the Catholic church because it was more of a social thing for me. To be honest, my family knew nothing about any particular religion. I liked to go and often, because I got to hang out with my friends and joke around.

"Holy crap!" I shout, my back arching as I jump forward, trying to get away from the cold buckets of water I'm being doused with. The stark difference between the cold water and my body temperature forces an uncontrollable shiver to roll through me. I'm now drenched from head to toe, wiping the water from my eyes as Joey laughs out loud from behind me. I already know what's coming next. Not having a second to spare, I take off in a full sprint, needing to escape about seven more of my friends as they come after me with cans of shaving cream.

This is only one of many summer games we play, but this one in particular uses cold buckets of water combined with shaving cream or whipped cream. The goal: to make a colossal mess of each other, but at least we're making this mess outside in the backyard. There are times, however, when we make this exact mess in my friend's basement, and the cleanup after a game takes forever.

I jolt to the right, faking the guys out as I zigzag just before darting back to the left, trying to throw them off my trail. Since I train for boxing, it requires miles of running, so I'm probably the fastest of the bunch, but the yard is only so big before I eventually get cornered.

Hitting a dead end near the row of hedges outlining the property, I shake my own can of shaving cream, hoping to get some guys before I get covered. I twist around while in midstride, with a glob of white, creamy foam in my hand, and just as I'm about to slap it onto Timmy's chest I'm lifted off my own two feet from behind.

Crap! He's got me! I'm not sure if there is such a thing as being tickled to death, but if there is, this would be it. All of my friends have ganged up on me, taking part in the action, because I've been made everyone's target. Four of my friends trip over each other, trying to tickle me as I get dragged away by a six-foot-tall giant. Everyone is hooting, hollering, and laughing, and I thank God I went to the bathroom before I came over here; otherwise, I would've pissed myself already.

I find myself being plunked down onto Father John Farrill's lap, his strong, steely legs wrapping around my body, pinning me in-between his thick thighs while his large hands slip underneath my wet T-shirt. The fabric clings tightly to my skin from being soaked with water, but with a firm grip, he's able to get my shirt half-off. In my struggles, I'm able to stop him from removing my shirt entirely, but my arms are stuck in the sleeves with my tee halfway over my head, trapping me. I squirm and twist in vain, needing to get away from the onslaught of what must be a hundred fingers tickling the sides of my ribs all the way up to my armpits.

Somehow, I manage to get my arms untangled from the clingy material, but not the way I wanted. My shirt's been ripped off, and sadly, I have no more control over my attackers now than when my arms were trapped.

Father Farrill runs his hands over my bare

stomach, lathering handfuls of shaving cream all over my body as he tickles me in-between. I can't breathe I'm laughing so hard. I'm flailing all over, trying to push everyone away with all my might, including the priest, but it's like trying to move a brick wall.

The tips of his strong fingers slip beneath the belt-line of my cut-off jeans as he then proceeds to undo my pants button. It's really no use—there is no escaping what's coming next. Nobody can match this beast of a man who's very muscular, unusually strong, and in great physical condition.

I'm able to contort my upper torso around, keeping him from being able to unbutton my shorts, and at the same time, I slap a handful of shaving cream over his cheek. The palm of my hand meets with his stubbly beard, the hairs so short they're prickly to the touch. I laugh harder when his eyes go wide with surprise, because usually the man is too quick and too strong for any of us to even come close to getting the upper hand. Although we always try, we rarely succeed in making a mess of him. Even when he's dressed in his white collar, like he is now, all bets are off and he's fair game to us all.

One of my friends—and I'm not sure who, because everything is a blur at the moment—manages to finally undo my jean shorts. Jerry and Kevin waste no time as they start tugging on the hem, attempting to pull them off me as I kick them away.

The point of the game, besides getting tickled and

mauled to death, waterlogged, and smeared with shaving cream head-to-toe, is to get stripped down while being trapped and tickled by everyone, including the priest. All of us kids are thinking these games are nothing but fun and laughter, and a great way to cool off in the hot summer's heat. There's nothing I can do to get out of this mess, my friends taking advantage of the situation just as I would them.

Whoever was chosen to be the target would first get chased down, and when finally caught, they'd get pinned down by the priest. He'd always have a chair he'd sit on while using all four of his limbs to keep us on his lap to entrap us, holding us captive. No matter how hard any of us kids tried, eventually we'd wind up stripped of our clothes, either down to our underwear or completely naked.

One by one, each piece of my sodden clothing finds its way off my body. I half-scream, half-laugh when a blast of water hits me like a fireman's hose with cold, sharp, biting pressure. The water hose—yet another implement in the priest's arsenal of weapons —would be used against us. Gobs of fresh shaving cream get slapped onto my exposed skin as everyone covers me in white foam, giving it their best shot to turn me into a snowman. The priest, of course, is fully justified to take part in this game, using the shaving cream and water as a diversion, an excuse to run his hands all over our naked bodies as the other kids help tickle and lather up the victim.

I wriggle between the priest's strong hold and the slippery substance of the foam, but the man's grip on me is still too strong for me to escape. I'm like a worm on a hot rock, squirming, contorting, and twisting myself by any means necessary to get loose. And because of all these erratic movements, I don't think twice about the placement of his hands as he tries to contain me, rubbing them all over my body. His fingers slip and slide through the thick lather, then oh-so-innocently down between my legs before they graze several times over my private parts.

The water games were all Father John Farrill's idea. He's been playing them for several years now. Everybody, including all the parents, thought this was a fantastic game, mainly because we were laughing, staying out of trouble, and having good, clean fun—or so we all thought. One would think living in New York and houses being on top of one another there would be neighbors who would be able to see all our shenanigans going on, but there were too many bushes and trees outlining this particular backyard, giving us privacy. Besides, even if someone did see us, they wouldn't have cared. We were just being boys and playing rough.

This was also the year of the streak. It was popular for people to run naked in public places so they could shock or amuse others. It was so widespread a song was made famous about the craze.

A few more minutes of torture, and I'm finally let

loose from the priest's hold. Half embarrassed, I scramble my naked ass away as quickly as possible, making a quick grab for my soaked clothes as they lay off to the side in a wet mound on the lawn. There's a lot of yelling and laughter filling the air, including my own, because this is Father Farrill, after all. He's just one of the guys, and he was always a great amount of fun.

He was always very good to us kids, and occasionally, he'd take us to the park and sometimes to the Yankees baseball games. Whenever the opportunity presented itself, he'd corral all the boys from the church, and because I was good friends with the family, I was always included. He loved baseball just like all of us. He was always telling us how he played minor league baseball in his younger years, but I knew better. I'd seen him throw a ball, and he couldn't throw one with any accuracy. I figured, because he knew all the families had athletic kids, he felt the need to brag, trying to fit in amongst us.

Breathing heavily from all the exertion, I tug my wet pants back on, and then wring out my T-shirt.

Out of the corner of my eye, I see Charlie rushing at me, so I quickly bend down and grab my can of shaving cream, getting ready for another onslaught. He holds up his hands in surrender, as he tells me excitedly, "Johnny! Guess what? Father Farrill says you can be an altar boy too!"

My brows crease in confusion. "What?" I ask

disbelievingly.

His blond hair has fallen in front of his eyes, and as he sweeps his wet strands off to the side, he repeats, "You can be an altar boy like us!"

Yes, I've been going to St. Thomas Church for quite some time and have known Father Farrill for several years now, but I'm confused. I look over at the priest and tilt my head. "But I'm not baptized," I tell him in a bewildered voice.

The priest waves me off with a smile. "Don't worry about it. We'll take care of that later."

I knew my friends really looked up to this man, but going to church was more about socializing for me, not becoming serious about God or religion. "I'm not even Catholic," I say more to myself than anyone, but the priest hears me.

"It's not a problem," he assures. "We can take care of all that with time."

~~*

I burst through our front door to find my father scouring over the newspaper, looking at the sports section. The second I enter the kitchen, his eyes meet mine then he tilts his chin down, looking over the rim of his glasses as he raises a brow in question, all without saying a word.

"Dad!" I blurt out eagerly and out of breath from

running all the way home. "Can I go with my friends and Father Farrill to see a movie?"

He puts his paper down on the kitchen table, giving me his full attention, before he asks, "What movie are you going to see?"

"It's called *Deliverance*." The second I tell him the name of the movie, my dad's eyes narrow, his forehead creasing at the brows.

"It's *what?*" he hisses, as if he didn't hear correctly. "You're going to see what?"

"We want to go see *Deliverance*. It's a movie," I repeat more clearly this time, and when I do, the look on his face tells me he isn't happy. I scratch the top of my head, wondering what I said wrong. I have no idea what the movie is about, but it sounded good to me when my friends explained it.

"No, no," he says, shaking his head in disbelief, and then he leans forward, placing his elbows on the table, as if getting closer to me will clarify things a bit more. "Are you sure that's the movie?"

"Yeah," I tell him with utmost certainty.

He sits back in his chair with a perplexed look on his face. "Something's wrong here," he murmurs, sounding very sure of himself. "Something's very wrong."

He pushes himself away from the table, the metal legs of the chair screeching across the wooden floor. He stands up and immediately makes his way to the living room. Highly curious of what he's up to, I follow behind him. He stops at the only phone we have as it rests silently on the credenza. I watch as he opens up our personal address book, which is full of family, friends, and neighbors' phone numbers.

His lips are thinned out, which is a dead giveaway that he's definitely upset. He's deep in thought, trying to process something in his head as he swipes the numbers on the rotary dial. Bringing the black phone receiver to his ear, he waits for the other line to be answered as he taps his finger on the table's surface.

"Yes, is Mr. O'Sullivan there?" he asks rather curtly. "This is Mr. Alite. I need to speak to your dad."

About a minute goes by, and then I hear a deep voice say "Hello" on the other end of the line.

"This fucking priest," my dad starts off in a heated tone, getting right to the point, but then he pauses as if he's been interrupted. I'm taken aback. Everyone knows my dad is unfiltered and that he's not religious, but I bet they sure as hell didn't expect this from him.

"I don't give a shit," he barks into the phone "I don't care if he's the pope! The guy is a fucking nut job!" My eyes snap open wide with surprise. It's a huge no-no to even think negatively about a priest, let alone talk about one like this, but my dad doesn't care.

"There's something wrong with him," he tells Mr. O'Sullivan with certainty. I can't make out what the other man is saying, but I don't think it's the answer my dad was looking for.

"Do you know what movie this fuck-face wants to take them to?" he shouts, and then after a short pause, he starts up again. "Are you nuts? Listen to what you're saying!"

For the next few minutes, each side seems to take turns, exchanging remarks I can only catch one-sided, but I can only imagine Mr. O'Sullivan is every bit as upset as my father.

"I'm telling you, this guy's a nut. He's full of shit." Another pause. "You want an instance? For one, this priest claimed he was a minor league Yankees ballplayer, for fuck's sake! What kind of priest feels the need to tell lies like that? And now he's wanting to take these kids to see *this* movie!" he says intensely, urging Mr. O'Sullivan to see his side of things. Since my father isn't religious, I believe he's able to see something none of us could, even though he doesn't know what that something is. He wasn't fooled like all the other parents.

"You should watch your kids around this man," my father warns. "He's always around them. Yeah— well… my kid ain't going to that." He then slams his hand on the table in front of him, adding, "You can be mad at me all you want. I call 'em how I see 'em, and something is wrong with this guy."

After my dad hangs up the phone, he turns and looks straight at me, speaking very firmly. "The guy is a jerkoff. I don't know what he's up to, but something is off. I don't trust him."

I give him a nod, understanding this is my father's way of letting me know I don't have to respect the man and is warning me to be on guard around him. After this incident, I plan on looking at the priest with very suspicious eyes. My dad is right; he was lying about knowing how to play baseball, as well as who he played for. So, if a man of God could lie about this, what else would he lie about?

It wasn't Father Farrill's charisma that made him so trusted; it was the fact he wore a collar. The way he played with us with the water and shaving cream was innocent to us. We didn't understand at that time in our lives, but in all actuality, the man was trying to molest us. We simply did not see things this way, and the parents didn't dare question this type of play. It was taboo to suggest that a priest would even have such a hidden agenda.

Chapter 13

Johnny Gebert and George Grasso, in my eyes, were two disloyal, uneducated, low-level street thugs. George had two brothers, Chris and Luis, who were part of the gang and they were no different..

The majority of the 7N9 Gang members were okay guys and the minority were garbage like Johnny Gebert. Those members who were degenerate were out of control, completely wild. They had morals like any two-bit junkie on the streets, with no care if they raped or robbed an innocent person. Guys like Johnny wanted to control our area. They sold drugs, robbed and beat people, and didn't hesitate to kill or maim anyone who got in their way. Most would turn on their own mother if they thought it meant earning a profit.

But there were also a select few who were decent guys, some like Timmy Donahue and George Catalano. They're great friends of mine, and very protective of the people who live in our neighborhood. Gang members like them just happened to be on the wrong path, but they were just like me in many ways, trying to make a buck and get out of our financial situation. Whether right or wrong, they were trying to find their way out of the streets, just like me.

The gang itself was far ahead of its time in regards to their aggressive and violent behavior. They carried knives and guns, not thinking twice about using them on anyone who challenged them, and at age sixteen, Johnny G. had already killed another kid.

My brother Jimmy and I were tough and aggressive, but we were just fighting with our hands. We didn't carry around weapons the way this gang did. My father was adamant about my brother and me standing on our own and not being part of any gang. He taught us that we didn't need a group of guys behind us in order for people to fear us.

My father was a great lecturer, constantly nagging us to do things like brush our teeth, all the way to more serious stuff. Every chance he got, he'd give us a talking to, saying, "Don't be a punk. Don't be part of the gangs. You can be friends with them, but don't join them." No matter what kind of pressure was put upon me or my brother to join, we resisted.

The two of us never wore jackets, or colors, and we only hung out with these guys on occasion. It was convenient to be friends with a lot of the gang members. We got the benefit of hanging out with them, but we were still able to maintain our independence. Kind of like what my father was doing with his own ties to the mafia. He was friends with a lot of gangsters, but wasn't part of their crew.

"Listen, I had a problem with Chris Grasso today," my brother informs me as we approach the J train. "We got into a bit of an argument in school. He was hoping he could intimidate me, and because he's involved with the gang, he thought I'd back down."

I give my brother a nod as I keep my eyes zoned in on the fifteen kids hanging around the train station who are part of the 7N9 Gang. They're marked by the bold Irish colors of orange and green patched onto their white-washed jean jackets. My friend Timmy's brother, Tommy, who's a gang member designed their jacket. Many of my close childhood friends had joined, but I never did. I was considered to be a chameleon on the streets, because I was known to be able to fit in and mingle with everyone from every type of background imaginable. I mixed in with sports friends, gangs, adults, mobsters; you named it, I could blend in.

I presume they've been waiting for my brother, and it's confirmed when Chris Grasso steps forward. The closer we get, the more tension fills the air, but we're brothers; we have each other's back, and we stand our ground to confront these guys head on. It's busy here, a lot of older people at the train station watching both sides with newfound interest.

What many kids don't realize is, even though Jimmy and I look like skinny punk kids, we know how to fight. My brother is bigger and tougher than me. He's also about five inches taller than me and better with his hands, and when it comes to fighting as a boxer, he has more natural talent.

Jimmy is well-adapted, able to play all types of sports. Both him and his close friend, Joe Galliano, are the ones in Woodhaven who have the most natural sports talent around.

Chris's eyes narrow as he makes a fist with one hand, punching it into his other as if it should intimidate us. "You gonna fight me," he snarls at Jimmy, trying to provoke him. "You think you're big and bad now. Let's see how you do against a gang."

His threats fall on deaf ears. I couldn't care less how many here are willing to fight. But some of the guys in the gang that we're friendly with step forward to interject. Timmy pushes a lock of blond hair from his eyes, as he sternly tells Chris, "Your problem is with Jimmy only. You want to fight, you fight him fair," he demands. "One on one."

Chris sizes my brother up and half laughs, thinking he's going to kick his ass within seconds. I keep a poker face, knowing the exact opposite is about to happen. The 7N9 Gang gather around in a semicircle, and some other spectators look on with curious interest.

Chris takes off his jacket and hands it to one of the guys in the gang who's standing beside him. He flexes his muscles to show off, and this time, I can't help but let a small flicker of a smirk pull on the corner of my lips. I'm so going to enjoy watching this kid struggle to remain on his feet.

I glance at Jimmy, who gives me a curt nod—his way of telling me he's got this in the bag—and then he steps forward to confront Chris. The guys surrounding us are already hooting and hollering, getting pumped up for a show. A few of our friends in the gang already know what's going to happen, but they too want to see Chris get knocked down a peg or two.

My brother is full of vigor and spirit. He's smooth, quick, and graceful on his feet—a real sight to behold when he's in action. Chris throws the first punch, but Jimmy ducks out of the way to deliver a swift, punishing left-handed blow to Chris's jaw just before he gives a harrowing hit to his gut.

"*Oomph*" is the sound that escapes Chris's lungs, and my brother pummels him from the get-go.

Jimmy is so adept, such a natural when it comes to boxing, that he's skill personified. The guys surrounding us shout aloud, trying to boost Chris's psyche, but it won't help; nothing is going to help this guy short of a miracle. The punches are as loud as drums, sounding like an intense heartbeat with flawless rhythm. It's the repeating sound of punches and jabs coming from my brother's handiwork. The guy never stood a chance. The beating is intense and is music to my ears.

I still stand by and at the ready, willing to jump in just in case someone gets the bright idea to step in with any kind of foul play to help Chris out.

My brother has no mercy on this kid, and if he were on the other end of my fists, I would've given him zero leeway either. He's getting everything that's been coming to him probably for a very long time now. It serves him right, the way he's been pushing around others. This time he tried to bully the wrong guy.

Despite the blood oozing from his nose and smearing across his face, I watch in sick delight as his face drains of color. Then his eyes roll back in his head, and all too soon, I know it's over. I smile, my brother having beat the fuck out of him with his bare hands.

Chris drops to the ground on all fours, spitting blood from his mouth as he tries to get his bearings on his hands and knees.

Timmy, my friend, steps in holding up his hands as if he's the contender of a pro boxing match. I smile with pride at my brother. I've always looked up to his skills and natural ability to fight gracefully. Jimmy's breathing heavily, but I think half of it is from the adrenaline rush, not the physical fight.

"It's over, guys," Timmy says with finality. He's not

telling the other gang members the fight is over; he's saying in very few words that these Alite brothers are tough, they fight, and they should be respected. Anyone would now think twice before screwing with us again. All except for George Grasso. It took him several times before he got the message.

~~*

I never fell into any one category or stereotype when it came to being trendy, following any particular bands or music genres such as punk, disco, or rock. I wasn't any of those things, never caring to follow any one individual or thing. I was my own person. Although, my brother was quick to point out I was becoming more and more wild and out of control.

I started getting stronger, bigger, more intense with every single thing in my life, including boxing and baseball. I don't know if other people felt threatened by this, or if they didn't want to see me excel, or if they were just that crazy and wild themselves. But I was having too many personal run-ins lately with George Grasso, and I was about to snap.

The rubber soles of my sneakers make a loud squeaking noise against the polished wooden floor in the main gym, echoing off the walls as I compete against Timmy Donahue for the basketball. With it being wintertime, we decided to shoot a few hoops of basketball after school. As I said, Timmy's a childhood friend of mine, and the fact he's been involved with the 7N9 Gang makes no difference to me. What I find amusing, though, is despite the gang not caring about their own members, they're actually scared of him. He's sturdy and burly, a tough fighter, and not to be messed with.

I snag the ball on the rebound and dribble a few times with my back to Timmy, keeping him from getting the ball. I twist and spring upward, making a shot.

"Yes!" I shout, ecstatic about my ten-foot shot.

"That was pure luck," he taunts as he grabs the ball. I grin at him, satisfied I'm only three points down. He's a great player, plus he has the advantage of being so tall, and as hard as I try, I can never beat him. We're working up a sweat and having a great time together, but all too soon, it comes to an abrupt halt.

As Timmy dribbles and I'm in defender position, a voice sounds out from behind us. "Why does everyone talk about the Alites like their so tough?" I pause, no longer caring about Timmy scoring. "All I see is a skinny-assed kid who couldn't fight his way out of a wet paper bag," the voice adds.

I'd like to think I'm not believing my ears, but I stop playing ball and turn around to see who is mouthing off.

"George Grasso," I sneer. I step forward and get in his face, noticing the one lazy eye he has, and ask,

"What are you looking *that* way for? You looking at me, or you looking the other way for your mother?" And then I start laughing.

Timmy lets loose a powerful belly laugh too, because he knows me like the back of his hand. He understands my looks are deceiving. He and his brother, Tommy, were always coming over to my house to wrestle with me and Jimmy. My brother and I are ripped-wired, meaning even though we're small, we're all muscle and no fat. Both of us are fast and exceptional with our hands.

George, who's wearing a contemptuous smirk, makes it evident he doesn't like my comeback. "Yeah —I'll fuck you up," he challenges me in a derisive tone.

It took all of a split-second to run up on him, getting in his face, as I challenge him back. "What'd you say?"

I guess he thought I was going to back down, because I see the quick flinch in his eyes before he recovers, acting as if my boldness has no effect on him. George is about the same height as me, but he's stockier. Regardless, he knows of me, but he doesn't know me well enough to be talking trash like this so brazenly.

"Whoa, whoa, whoa," Timmy says, trying to take charge, wanting to diffuse the situation as he slips his thick body in-between us. "What's the problem here?"

I give a noncommittal shrug, and reply, "Hey, no

problem." But then my temper gets the best of me, and before I know it, I'm slapping George with a lot of force to the side of his head.

"Who the fuck you think you are?" he yells just as he reaches behind his back to pull out a decent-sized knife.

He waves it behind Timmy's back, who's yelling at him, "Put the knife away, you dumbass."

I lift my chin in defiance and look George straight in his crazy eyes, telling him point-blank and full of confidence, "You're not doing nothin' with that knife." Even though I show him no fear, I'm a little bit nervous about his knife, but he isn't going to intimidate me. I stand my ground.

Timmy is talking double-time, trying to convince George to put the knife away. Even after school, there are too many teachers floating around the hallways of the school, keeping a lookout for trouble.

"Let's take this somewhere else," Timmy suggests, pointing down the long corridor to the locker rooms. "You want to fight him," he says to George, "then let's move it down in the hallway where nobody can see. Too many teachers hanging around. It's quiet down by the bathrooms. There ain't nobody down there."

He gives a curt nod in acknowledgment, and then the three of us start heading down the hallway to duke it out. As I'm getting myself pumped up for the fight, I can see by the look in George's eyes that he's starting to have second thoughts. It's clear he's one of those guys full of bravado—and full of shit. Guys like him are all talk, and I'm thinking that, because his older brothers are in the 7N9 Gang too, he's using their reputation to bully and subdue others, but it won't work on me.

I'm not scared of the Grasso name. Hell, his brother Louis already tried to rob me at the train station a couple years back. He pulled out a long knife, thinking he could take advantage of me. All it did was leave a lot of animosity and bad blood in its wake.

My eyes narrow on George. He's already trying to figure a way out of this, but I'm not interested in that. Timmy knows me too well; he knows I'm not going to back out, no matter what. He's aware of my fighting history.

The one thing I do understand is that Timmy is somewhat caught in the middle of us. For one, he's part of the 7N9 Gang and has an allegiance to them, but he's also my lifelong friend. But since he knows me personally, he knows I can fend for myself just fine. There's no doubt in Timmy's mind that I can pummel George to the ground in seconds.

In our neighborhood, if somebody wants to fight, you're not supposed to step in on that, and you don't back down from a challenge, no matter what. If you're challenged, you have to fight.

With George trying to find a way to back out, as a

last-ditch effort, he sticks his hand out for me to shake. I look at him as if he's lost a marble. "I'm not shaking your hand," I tell him firmly.

Timmy butts in, encouraging me, "John, shake his hand."

I shift my eyes only, making sure to keep a close watch on George and his knife. "Fuck that, I'm not shaking his hand," I grit out.

I know the boy isn't going to fight now, so I start walking away, and as I do, George says from behind, "Come on, I was just playing with you."

I pause midstride and twist to look over my shoulder, giving him a half-laugh that screams of pure mockery and says, *"Yeah... okay, you coward."* At the same time, a surge of anger surfaces out of nowhere. My jaw muscles flex, as I add between clenched teeth, "Don't you ever try to fuck with me again."

Surprisingly, his hard head finally got the message after that. He never tried to mess with me again after the incident. Sadly, George's family were all fucked-up in the head. All of them used guns, knives, and drugs, which made my brother and me probably look like really nice kids.

The one thing nobody could wrap their heads around was the lack of fear we had, because we'd never back down from anything. We'd die before we'd let anyone push us around.

Chapter 14

$\mathbf{A}$ high level of edginess is in the air as we walk through the multilevel parking garage in south Bronx. We've been here too many times to count, but tonight is not one of our typical outings. I can feel the tension rolling off my father and Bobbi in droves. I already know Bobbi is strapped with a pistol, needing to be prepared for anything. If my father is, he doesn't say, and I know enough not to ask. He turns around, his voice low and tight. "You need to pay attention to everything around you tonight. Be on high alert."

My father fears nothing in this life, and he's taught me to be the same way. So, in order for him to say something like this, it means the probability for danger to occur is very high. His words make me take pause, waking me up to the full reality of the situation. An interesting thing about my father is that he's never treated me like a kid, even when I was little. He would never baby me; instead, he trained me for the real world from the get-go, talking to and treating me as if I were an adult.

"I got it, Dad," I tell him with conviction.

"Pay attention, watch everything around you, and let me know about anything you're not sure of."

I give him a quick nod, already scoping out our surroundings with an eagle eye.

We approach a beat-up steel door that's seen better days, as a man who's standing guard begins to unlock the lock-bar that stretches across the doorframe. A small space had been sequestered off from the parking garage we're in. It's enclosed by concrete walls, creating a unique hideaway for men who indulge in street gambling.

The three of us walk inside the small cubicle, and once we're in, the door slams shut behind us. We're locked inside a concrete box that acts as a freezer in the winter and a hot box in the summer, and once you're locked in, you're stuck. There is no going in or out unless someone opens a door for you. Even if the police were able to get through the first set of doors, there would be no way they'd get past the second.

With steel doors on either side of us, I look up at the camera in the upper corner of the ceiling... waiting. I glance to my left to see a bead of sweat roll off Bobbi's forehead. It's not from nerves, but from the hot, stagnant summer air. He's got to be hotter than me by far, because he's wearing a sports coat to hide his pistol. Under the scrutiny of the camera, it would be normal protocol for one to take off their jacket, open their shirt, and whatever else one has to do in order to pass inspection before being allowed in. But the men on the other side of the door don't dole out these instructions. Tonight is different; these men already know why we're here, plus they've known my father for decades.

The three of us are wound tight, but I'm this way because all I want to do is have my father's back, making sure nothing bad happens to him. I know he's anxious, because he's grown unusually quiet. He gets this certain look about him when he's uptight that tells me he's in concentration mode, worrying whether or not things are going to play out smoothly or not.

I look up at the peephole in the door we're about to go through, and then I hear the lock disengage on the all-steel bar that's bolted on the inside of the other room. This is the place everyone calls Under the Umbrella. It's a typical backroom gambling spot for wise guys, and this place specifically has been here for decades.

Passing their code of approval, the door swings open and we're allowed into the clandestine room. Upon crossing over the threshold, the air conditioning pushes air my way, bringing along with it the familiar smell of booze and stale tobacco. At first glance, the scene before me should feel ominous, testing one's nerves with the room being filled with gangsters, but I've known most of these men for over half my life.

I've always been enthralled by everything that has transpired here. To be privy to and allowed to be part of this closed society has been nothing short of exciting. When I was a little kid of six, I knew exactly what kind of establishment I was walking into. But even now, at fourteen, I don't fully comprehend what this life is truly about. I'm only seeing things in one dimension, only being exposed to the glamorous side, and a witness to the fancy suits, expensive cars and cigars, and gorgeous women. I always looked forward to coming here with my dad, and much of the time, it'd give me an adrenaline rush just to see these men in action.

"Hey, Little Matty," Al calls out, his thick Italian accent booming over the noise of multiple conversations going on at the same time. I took after my old man in looks, so it's only fitting I got nicknamed after my father, Matthew. I look past several gangsters, and once my eyes adjust to the dim lighting and the billowing clouds of smoky cigar haze, I immediately smile when I spot Al. For a short, stocky guy, he's a mighty powerful man, one who has a lot of pull in his world. Having spent so much time here over the years, I would hear stories when Al wasn't around about how dangerous he is. Everyone's afraid of him, thinking he's a nut, but I love him.

Al was really good to me. He was always going out of his way to make sure I was looked after. He would order the guys around him to get me some ice-cream, or whatever they had in their little kitchen when I arrived. It was through Al specifically that I learned I could be nice and gentle, and at the same time, I could also be very dangerous if someone disrespected my kindness. Being kind in the streets was frowned upon; it was considered weakness. I learned those lessons firsthand, but by watching Al, I understood I didn't have to be an animal to be respected.

Weaving through the men and the few junky old card tables, I spy Good-Looking Jack. He's probably the wealthiest of all the men. He's a big wise guy, but one whom most everyone likes, and obviously, very handsome. Al greets me with a kiss to each side of my cheek and gives me a quick hug. "How ya doin', kid?"

"Great. I'm in the lineup for Junior Olympics," I tell him, excited about the progress I've made in boxing since I got picked up by a trainer not too long ago.

"Outstanding. When's the fight?" he asks, slapping me on the back.

"Two weeks from now." I've been training my ass off for it too. After my workouts and sparring, I'd run ten miles at least four days a week.

Al gives me a proud grin then looks to his left, and orders with authority, "Hey, Vinny, get the kid some ice-cream, will ya?"

Vinny stands from the card table, leaving his game without a word. I follow him into the tiny kitchen, letting Al get back to his game. I always get a nostalgic feeling when I'm here. I look at the kitchenette table for two and grin. Many nights I shared that very table with my brother while my dad and uncle gambled the night away, sometimes from ten at night to six in the morning. It was exciting when the guys would invite us out of the kitchen, allowing us to hang out and watch them play cards.

I sit down in the rickety wood chair and watch Vinny open the small refrigerator. It's very dated, one like you'd see on *The Honeymooner's* show. This hangout is very small in square footage, and the entire place is rundown and dilapidated, but it's a man's man kind of place. There's a jukebox with an inch of dust on top, pushed off into one of the corners. It's been there ever since I've been coming here, but no one ever turns it on.

The major game tonight is 3-Card Monty. I know this, because there are a lot of Spanish guys here. I was told this game's origin comes from Spain. From the angle I'm sitting, I can see Uncle Harry's six-one frame leaning over the table as he deals out cards. I never get to interact with him when he's running the place, except on the rare occasion he can grab a five-minute break. He's all about business anyway, and judging from the crowd tonight, he's probably going to bring in a lot of money. He's the one who oversees the entire operation here. I sit back and eat, admiring Uncle Harry's ability to move cards with such precision and ease. I grin thinking about one of his best traits, which is counting cards.

Ever since I can remember, Uncle Harry has always dressed like a gangster. Even though he could never be a made man because of our Albanian heritage, he was a really big earner. He always drove big Caddys and Lincolns. So I knew what he was and who he was from an early age. It wasn't like a hidden fact, the ones who were gangsters in our family—we all knew who they were.

One thing is obvious tonight. Bobbi and my dad aren't here to play cards. They're here for one purpose only—to handle a business transaction. This much I do know.

Finished with my ice-cream, I toss the Styrofoam bowl and plastic spoon into the trash and step out from the kitchen. I pause midstride as Al suddenly bolts up so fast his chair topples behind him, the metal seat making a loud clanking sound against the concrete floor. The room has fallen deathly quiet. He's seething mad about something, the tension so thick I could cut it with a knife.

I've never seen Al act this way before. In fact, I don't remember anyone ever losing their shit in this room before. These men have always kept their emotions in check, just as they would by wearing their poker face during these card games. It's always been the rules of this place that if a guy has beef with another, they're supposed to take it outside. But as quickly as things are transpiring, I'm not sure Al is going to make it outside. He's got a grip on the cheap cardboard table so tight I swear he could snap it in two with a simple flick of his wrists.

I've always known there to be tension between Al and Good-Looking Jack, but what I'm seeing right now brings their relationship to a new level of hate, and out in the open. Good-Looking Jack glances over at me, and if he's shaken by Al's display of aggression, it doesn't show. His voice is calm and measured as he looks me square in the eye, and says, "You look surprised, Matty. Surely this isn't the first time you're seeing your pal Al in action, is it?"

"Leave the kid out of this," Al snaps. My eyes dart between the two men, and I wonder how, all of a sudden, I wound up in the middle of their conflict.

"Take a good look," Jack warns. "Could be you someday." He's trying to bait Al, this much is clear. I don't know what is going on between them, and maybe I never will, but I can't imagine what Jack has done.

Al steps off to the side of the card table, his hands balled into fists, and for a moment, I think he's going to pummel Jack, which would be a grave mistake. Al would be asking for a death sentence if he puts his hands on him. Everybody knows made-guys from any group can't touch each other, not unless they get permission from the higher ups first.

With his chest heaving with unspent rage, he grits out the words between clenched teeth. "You've got real nerve, you son of a—"

"That's enough!" Old Man Mike shouts, cutting Al off. His thunderous voice effectively slices through the men's banter, silencing the entire room. The air of the room quickly shifts, filling with unease and disquiet as all heads have turned, focusing on the authority in the room, which is Mike.

"Let it go, Al," Mike warns, his eyes full of heat narrowed on his son-in-law. Mike being Al's father-in-law is one thing, but he's also the captain of the Luchesse family, which means everybody is supposed to do what Mike says. And even though Blackie, Uncle Harry, and Jack own this place, Old Man Mike is still the authoritative figure when he's around, simply because he outranks everyone.

To be honest, Blackie doesn't have to take orders from Mike, because he's a Gambino guy, but it's a respect thing. He's still going to respect Mike for his position within *The Life*. Besides, Mike is a fair man; he's not one to throw his weight around, but rest assured, he will control his own men. If things happened to get out of hand, it'd be like a slap in Blackie's face for losing control in his own place. So, I imagine Mike stepped in for this reason.

I stand here frozen, just like everyone else in the room. My heart is pounding so hard in my chest I'm wondering if anyone else can hear it besides me. I'm rattled on the inside, but I've learned over the years to wear my own poker face, and show no emotion.

For the first time ever, I'm seeing Al's hostile nature in action, and if looks alone could kill, Jack would've already been dead by now. Al turns around and hastily picks up his chair, every muscle in his body wrought with tension. Clearly, he's not happy about being shut down, but he knows better than to say anything more. I can now understand what the other men were talking about, and why they fear Little Al.

I can't fathom why he holds so much enmity toward Jack. Everybody, and I mean *everybody*, likes Jack. He's a good guy, full of class, and he's definitely not a killer. Unlike Al. That much is obvious.

One man throws a few chips into the center of the card table, upping the ante in hopes of defusing the situation. I guess it works, because one by one the men turn back around, cards in hand, and the games resume. I glance over at Uncle Harry, who's already started dealing out cards again, and I'm in awe of how quickly everybody gets right back to business as if nothing ever happened.

My father and Bobbi are looking ill at ease. They're keyed up, and judging from their stiff postures, they're more than ready to leave. I gladly make my way toward the door, ready to leave myself. I watch as Blackie pats Bobbi on the back, whispering something in his ear as he hands over a large duffle bag.

"Do me a favor and walk them out to the car, will ya?" Mike instructs Al.

"Sure, boss," Little Al replies calmly. Amazingly, he's already got his emotions in check. Al stands up and jerks his chin toward a couple of tough-looking Spanish guys, giving them an unspoken signal. The men scoot their chairs back then stand to their full height, both with cigars hanging out of their mouths. As the three of them follow us out through the secure doors and to the car, they remain silent, looking every bit the part of armed and dangerous gangsters.

Reaching Bobbi's Monte Carlo, Little Al kisses my father on each cheek then mine, as Bobbi slips into the driver side and shuts the door. He's not about to stay idle with a bag of cash in his hands.

"Matty." Little Al's voice is full of concern, as he tells my father, "Be careful." He briefly glances at me, the look of worry in his eyes palpable, giving me pause. My father gets in the front passenger seat as I slip into the back. There's a new level of danger I feel vulnerable to as Bobbi starts the car and we begin to pull away. I turn around in the oversized bench seat and look out the rear window, my gut instincts telling me we have to be extra vigilant, watching our side-view and rearview mirrors as if our lives depend on it.

Bobbi tosses the large canvas bag over the seat as we leave the parking garage, saying, "Look what's in here, Johnny."

The overstuffed bag lands heavy in my lap as I grab ahold of it and unzip it with much curiosity. "Wow!" I exclaim loudly the second my eyes land on stacks and bundles of cash, each thick wad neatly held together by paper bands.

"You know how much money is in there?" Bobbi asks with excitement.

I look up at him. "No."

"A million dollars in cash," he answers with a grin.

My eyes go huge. "Really?" I'm awestruck. I'm used to handling a few thousand at a time, gambling on behalf of my father, but never in my life have I seen this amount of money. I glance down at all the green bills in my possession, not sure what a million dollars is supposed to look like. "Are you sure?"

Getting a kick out my reaction, Bobbi's grin spreads into a full smile. "Well, you're gonna be counting it all out when we get home to make sure it's all there."

"What are you guys gonna do with it?" I ask, wondering how far a million bucks could go. My dad continues to be extra quiet, which means he's still on edge, but Bobbi is excited.

"Your father, me, Harry, and Blackie are purchasing and renovating an old shopping center. We're turning it into a nightclub. Gonna call it Hammerheads."

"Wow" is all I can manage to say.

"Blackie and your Uncle Harry are the ones who secured the money for us," he tells me proudly. I find it somewhat comical that Bobbi is a retired cop—a dirty cop—and his father-in-law, who's almost a police chief, is a straight-laced cop and knows nothing of Bobbi's illicit deals. Then I almost laugh out loud thinking about Uncle Harry. Leave it to him to be able to acquire this much money. He always made jokes that he's making more money a year than Reggie Jackson, and judging by the amount of money I'm holding in my hands, I believe him.

This is crazy! Yet I'm giddy with excitement, wondering if I'll ever get the opportunity to handle this much money on my own someday. I run my hands through the stacks of bills one last time before zipping up the bag.

Remembering Al's words, I place the bag on the floor and immediately begin watching cars and looking at people, paying extra attention to my surroundings. This could turn into something very dangerous... yet I'm not scared. I'm far from it. I'm more concerned about someone trying to take the money away from my father, or worse, shoot him.

Little did I know at this time just how ruthless and greedy the mafia was, nor was I aware of the extent to which they ran the city. Later, I would find out that this era in the seventies and eighties was considered the golden age for the mafia. Those in *The Life* had already put big plans into motion, infiltrating and controlling every legitimate business possible. From construction, trucking, the ports, garbage, food markets, unions, and more.

Those who dominated with corrupt power had the

ability to let you see what they wanted you to see, and all I saw was the exterior, the glamour of it all. I couldn't see them for what they truly were—a pack of rats who devoured anything in sight out of an insatiable hunger, willing to consume their own kind just to get ahead.

Even though I might not be consciously aware of the influence and amount of mob exposure I was subjected to, subconsciously I know I'm dealing with serious levels.

So, yet another mixed message was given to me by my father. I can hear him saying right now, *"I ain't hurting nobody. I ain't doing anything wrong. It's just gambling."*

I'm friends with some of these gangsters, yet he's telling me not to be involved with them because they're all no good, but every time I turn around, he's doing business with them. Being an adult, he can separate the two, and he doesn't understanding that I can't.

So here I am, holding a million bucks in my lap, yet our family is running around with holes in our shoes.

Chapter 15

I was nonstop, sometimes skipping school, or playing sports right after, but one thing always remained the same, my training. Five days a week, from six to eight-thirty at night, I wind up taking two buses then walk about fifteen blocks to get to the boxing gym. Gym time usually comes after two-to-three hours of baseball practice first. My weekends aren't free either. Saturday and Sunday, I'm in our basement, working out with punching bags, pull-up bars, and jump ropes, and sometimes a sparring match. Somehow, I manage to run ten miles four days a week on top of my already full schedule. I never stop training—never.

Boxing dominates my life every second of every day, but I'm in top mental and physical condition, and I'm more ripped than ever before. I've been more than ready to take my boxing to the next level.

Walking into the shopping center off Queens

Boulevard is like walking through a major thoroughfare, but it's the only way to get to the gym. As soon as I pass Alexander's store, I push through the next set of doors that has YMCA etched into the glass. It's either six steps up to the basketball courts or six steps down to the gym the second I walk through these doors. The courts and the gym always stay busy and packed.

Knowing I won't be allowed to have any water when we train, I head upstairs first, stopping at the water fountain first to drink my fill. The coaches are of the opinion we shouldn't drink a drop of water during our training, and it's miserable to be so dehydrated, and the muscle cramps are wicked. The coaches are very strict about this rule, and everyone who's training literally has to beg for permission to use this very water fountain, as it's the only one in the building.

It isn't just the boxing coaches who believe you shouldn't drink water while you're working out; it's that way with all sports. It's believed that, for whatever reason, drinking water while sweating and working out will give you pneumonia from the combination.

The echoes of screeching sneakers begin to fade as I make my descent downstairs to start my training. I'm accosted by the same smell that grabs me day in and day out. It's a funky smell of heat, sweat, and body odor, which fuses together, creating an aroma in the air that sticks in the back of your throat as if you're about to swallow a bowl of dog shit, and it never goes away.

This gym has been here since my father and uncle were kids. So that makes over forty years' worth of funk and stench that have permanently leached through the walls, creating the never-ending odor. But you know you're in a real gym—a man's gym—by the stink, the grime, and the endless swearing.

I stifle a laugh as I hit the main floor of the boxing facility, as Vic's loud, boisterous voice booms across the room, loud and clear. "If you're in my gym, you're gonna be a fighter," Vic says adamantly. "You ain't gonna train outside the ring either. I want you inside the ring."

As I make my way toward the locker room, I can already see Vic is on the move, getting ready to instigate trouble with one of the weightlifters as he stalks toward the ring with purpose.

Vic's naturally loud and gruff voice was intimidating enough at times, but he also stood over six feet tall, had rock-solid muscles, and a physique that didn't make him look his age of sixty-five. It was his gray, balding, and thin hair that gave his age away. Vic never did go pro, but he was a great fighter and coach.

"Hey, you insecure punk," Vic barks to a weightlifter who's leaning on the ropes, watching one of our boxers.

It already drives him nuts that these lifters had to

walk through the boxing area in order to get to the back part of the building to reach their weights. It's a hardcore gym, and the guys are huge, but even that doesn't deter Vic from giving them grief. In fact, he enjoys starting shit with them, getting some sort of sick pleasure from knocking these tough guys down. He has no patience when it comes to them.

"Why don't you hold your arms up like a boxer for three minutes?" Vic challenges in his thick New York accent. I stop for a moment and set my gym bag down, wanting to see how this plays out, because I already know it's going to be pure entertainment.

The big guy lets go of the ropes and turns to face Vic fully. He then stands at his full height, puffing out his broad chest, as if doing that would intimidate Vic. "Why do I need to do that?" he asks in a challenging tone. "If I were in this ring, I'd destroy that kid," the guy says, tilting his head to the side in the direction of Caesar, who's shadowboxing in the ring.

This is one of the major problems with overconfident weightlifters like this guy. They'd always watch small, skinny kids like me and size us up, thinking we have no strength or power. I'm not muscular; I'm skinny, but I'm ripped, and I know how to fight. I also have the endurance to last in the ring.

Apparently this guy makes a comment that Vic happens to overhear, and now he's become Vic's next target. He lives for these guys to mouth off in his gym, because he loves to challenge them, embarrass them, and then hand them their asses while the entire gym dies laughing.

This is actually a weekly scene with him calling out the weightlifters. He hates these guys near the boxing ring, even if they just want to watch. Vic thinks they're all punks, arrogant, and insecure, and if they open their mouth, it's all over. He'll abuse them even more and tell them to get in the ring, and when he tells them that, he's not giving these guys a choice. There's no backing out, and if they try, Vic embarrasses them even more. The shame of cowering is far worse than getting physically beaten down, and believe me when I say Vic is very capable of making them feel like cowards.

"Is that right, balloon boy? You think you could destroy my fighter?" Vic says, his voice full of mockery. A chuckle escapes me. Seeing Vic ride these guys is the highlight of everyone's day who trains here.

"Balloon boy?" the guy asks, half confused and half offended. "What the hell is that?"

"Because you're full of hot air. You couldn't fight your way out of a wet paper bag." All of us who train under Vic burst out with laughter at his quick and witty comebacks. These guys are huge power lifters, and they do get big and bulky, but Vic calling him this name is his way of putting him down, calling him weak.

"Okay." The guy shrugs arrogantly. "I'll fight the

kid, but I won't hit him too hard. I don't want to hurt him."

"It's okay," Vic says, his voice full of sick satisfaction. "You go as hard you want—how about that?" Vic nods to the boy's thick biceps, adding, "You look strong enough. So you do what you want." I can see Vic trying his damnedest to hide his smile, but all of us who know him know it's a foretelling of the humor to come.

Vic waves his arm in the air, calling for someone to glove up his newest sucker. I shake my head and laugh under my breath. This guy's pride will be his downfall today. "Hey, blockhead," Vic says with a devious grin, "put this headgear on that blockhead of yours."

Curiosity starts to draw a crowd; even the weightlifters come out of their weight room to watch the fight. They are all thinking that, because their friend is huge—a modern day Goliath—he'll be able to destroy Caesar. None of them have a clue what's in store for this guy, and those who do stand in silence with a smile on their faces.

By now, I've made my way to the ring, wanting a front-row view of what's about to go down. So, as this guy is getting geared up, I watch as Vic slips into the ring to talk to Caesar. Vic says in a low, deep voice so only a select few can hear, "Destroy this guy from the first second the bell sounds." Caesar nods with a devious grin on his face. "I want to see you on him relentlessly... until you knock him out," he adds.

Then Vic turns around in the ring, and shouts out, "You know how to dance, balloon boy?" The guy twists around and looks at Vic in confusion. "You know... box dance?" But all of us who box know exactly what Vic is referring to. He's being sarcastic. "What kind of music do you like to dance to? Ballet, pop, disco, rock? Because I think you're going to be better off with marching band music so you can march out of the ring before I need to call the EMS."

Guffaws, howls, and deep, rich laughter fill the entire downstairs gym like never before.

"Come on, two left feet. Get on in the ring. Show me what you got," Vic taunts, summoning him to the ring. Caesar starts dancing around with a wide grin on his face, waiting for the show to begin. He's only about five-foot-six and 170 pounds, and this weightlifter is about 220 pounds and six feet tall. Anyone who doesn't know about the sport, they would think this lifter has the fight in the bag, but what he doesn't know is that Caesar is turning pro. He's about twenty and really good.

The guy gets up, slips between the ropes, and gets in the ring, all while looking highly confident.

"Okay, balloon boy, get in there. Let me see what you're made of." Vic gives Caesar a wink that only a select few of us can see, and those of us who train under Vic know what that means. These guys haven't a clue that one minute in the ring is exhausting; plus, they don't know how to move.

The bell finally dings, and us boxers have a sadistic rush of self-satisfaction rolling through us as we wonder just how many seconds it'll take before this huge man drops to his knees in agony.

When they both come together, Caesar unleashes every bit of skill and power he possesses on the guy. I laugh aloud when I see the giant of a man try to counterpunch. I'm holding my stomach I'm laughing so hard. It's not like the guy is even throwing a regular punch. He's like a spastic girl on crack, every punch misdirected and wobbly, never hitting his target.

Caesar is one big blur of nothing but moves and red gloves flying through the air with precision and speed. The loud thwacking of his pummeling fists against this guy's body is an endless beat, sounding out like rhythmic drums in a fast rock song. It's complemented by short bursts of "*oomphs*" and a series of low, guttural grunts of agony.

Having lost his composure, Vic turns his back on the fight for a brief second, doubling over in laughter. He's so cracked up he swipes away the tears of laughter from the corners of his eyes.

I think it takes less than sixty seconds before this guy goes down. Vic shows no mercy, as he yells out to the guy, "You think maybe you're going too easy on him there? You know, your face has hit his hands like, what, thirty times already? Maybe you should go harder on your punches."

The guy is trying to quit, and it hasn't even been three minutes yet, which makes this situation even funnier. He crawls on his hands and knees, trying to make his way from the middle of the ring to the edge, in hopes of slipping out from between the ropes, but Vic won't let him out, not until he begs, because this is Vic.

"No, no, no," Vic starts off, shaking his head as he leans in closer to the guy. "It's okay; don't hold back." He puts him down at the same time he falsely encourages him. "What's the matter? Are you wearing left shoes on both of your feet? Is that the problem?"

I can see the look of defiance and contempt on the guy's face for being ridiculed in front of an entire gym. So he gets back up with newfound determination, thinking this revived adrenaline rush of anger will be enough to carry him through the first round. He's wrong—very wrong.

Caesar is given the signal to finish the guy off with a simple nod from Vic. Punch after punch is delivered to the man's face and gut. It's a relentless pounding, a one-sided fight, where this guy is merely in the ring as a human punching bag. His weightlifter friends are yelling, trying to cheer him on, but the encouragement is a lost cause. It's a sight to see—this grown man full of muscle wobbling and continually stumbling backward with each blow he's receiving from someone half his size.

The guy is struggling to remain upright, and I can

see the determination that was once in his eyes is now gone. His step falters, and he doubles over. He struggles to remain upright, but can't hold out any longer. Going down on all fours, he gasps for air over and over again, and it's plain to see he's finished; he doesn't want to get back up any more and fight.

"All right, all right. Hurry up," Vic intervenes again, not done poking fun at him. "Come on, get up. You've had enough rest." I burst out with laughter as all of us do who box, loving the way Vic is able to push the big guys around. "C'mon, finish up. You're really hitting him hard with your head. You're gonna bust his hand any second now!"

Then Vic gives Caesar a silent nod, telling him without words to go ahead and finish him off, and Caesar does just that.

The way the guy was acting, I thought he was going to throw up on the platform. He was gagging the entire time. But now, it's worse, and everybody's laughing their asses off as the guy dry heaves.

His face is beet red, and Vic continues to yell at him at the same time he's gagging, "Don't you throw up in my fucking ring!"

The guy holds his stomach, making all kinds of gestures, trying to keep his shit together. He didn't even make it one round.

It's a pathetic sight, but an oh-so-humorous one, to watch this heavy weightlifter swaying on all fours as he claws at the floor of the boxing ring, trying to get away from Caesar. He finally makes it to the edge of the ring, but Vic makes sure he's right there in front him, preventing him from getting out.

Vic leans down and says something to him, and I watch as the guy hangs his head for a moment, a look of anguish on his face. "C'mon, man," he says pleadingly.

Vic shakes his head, refusing to let him out—not until he admits his defeat in one of the most humiliating of ways. "Say it," Vic demands.

The guy lifts his chin and stares Vic in the eyes. I'm pretty sure he would admit to anything at this point just to escape the torture. His voice is croaky, half choked up, because he's gagging in-between his words. "Weightlifters are as tough as ballet dancers."

Everybody outside the ring, including all of the weightlifters, burst out with wild and boisterous laughter. The booming guffaws could probably be heard out on the main street we're so loud. My own stomach hurts from so much laughter, and I know, without a doubt, I'll remember this particular scene for the rest of my life. I also know Vic will abuse him and others like him nonstop for months to come.

Vic moves aside, chuckling and flashing a wide smile as he watches the guy clamor his way out of the ring. He's doubled over, holding his stomach and still gagging from getting too many punches to the gut.

Vic will never have mercy on these weightlifters— never. He yells in that rough voice of his, "Don't you throw up on my fucking floor!" He points toward the locker rooms. "The bathroom's are that way, balloon boy."

We all watch, wondering if the guy is going to make it to the bathroom in time as he zig-zags toward the men's locker room, gagging the entire way. Vic calls out behind him, "And weights go back in the backroom. That's where you belong!"

These were some of the best times of my life, moments like these. The fraternity of the boxing life, the camaraderie of my family and friends, and the spirit of humor.

Chapter 16

"**J**ust one time… all you gotta do is hit it one time," Vic deceitfully spurs on yet another weightlifter who thought he was God's gift to the muscle world. "If you can hit this double end bag with your right fist… just once… you'll win a prize." Vic's enthusiasm for taunting the weightlifters and wanting to make a spectacle of them always catches everyone's attention, drawing a large crowd every time.

The double end bag is not an easy thing to hit. There's a rubber type of rope that goes through the middle of this punching ball with either end secured from the floor to the ceiling. The ball remains at about chest height, and when pushed or punched, it then moves rapid and haphazard back and forth and side to side, vibrating and bouncing all over the place. It then becomes a real challenge to hit, even for the experienced.

As this muscle-bound guy tries to hit the bag,

everyone laughs around him, as Vic taunts, "Listen...
I told you... all you have to do is hit it one time."

I can see it in the man's eyes; he's trying hard to
focus on the moving target, his muscles taut with
frustration, wanting so bad to prove Vic wrong, that
he can do it. His right fist surges forward, missing
again for probably the tenth time, and with each miss,
Vic and everyone around him laughs even harder.

"You big dummy," Vic says between bouts of
laughter, "you couldn't hit the broad side of a barn if
you ran into it."

The guy throws his hands up in the air and shakes
his head, uttering a few curse words under his breath,
and I know he's done. Of course, Vic can't let him
walk away without ridiculing him as he leaves.

"Hey, maybe you'd have better luck at jumping
rope," Vic calls out behind him with a grin. I chuckle,
knowing these guys aren't able to jump rope, not even
a little bit, which would then earn them the name of
"two left feet."

I finish gearing up for my own fight tonight,
which involves me going up against a former Junior
Olympic champ. Jay is a Russian kid who'd won in our
weight class last year, and he's been knocking me all
over the place for the past month. One of the main
reasons for that is because he's been professionally
trained.

Being from the streets, I didn't have a professional
trainer who'd give me their undivided attention, and I

had never been in the ring with anyone in my weight class who was this good before. I know I'm not a polished fighter. All I know to do is to keep moving forward and get hit.

I guess that kind of relentless spirit is one that is not found every day. This mindset of mine caught the attention of a former pro-boxer named Nick, who then approached me, wanting to train me for the Junior Olympics. The past couple of weeks, he's been having me focus on counterpunches.

What I lack in skill, I make up for with speed, and the one thing Jay couldn't do was knock me down. I was frustrating him, especially because it didn't bother me how many punches he was getting in. This made him believe he wasn't hurting me, but he was; I just didn't show it. There was no way for him to know that pain lost its effect on me years ago. So despite the amount of physical suffering I endured at his hands, I just kept going back for more. That's how I was taught to fight.

But the coaches would laugh at me, because I was just getting hit so much, which wasn't a good thing. No matter what, I just went forward, never backward. My trainer loved this about me, but he had to teach me to move my head more, bob and weave, up and down, and dodge side to side.

The past few fights I've had with Jay, I was finally starting to get the upper hand, and I didn't realize it was chipping away at his self-confidence. I just recently qualified for the Junior Olympics pre-fight, which will take place in the Bronx only a week from now. Winning this pre-fight would advance me to fight in the Junior Olympics, and I can't even describe the excitement I'm feeling over this.

I was training like crazy, which oddly had my father concerned, because in his eyes, we could never train enough. Yet even he was worried I was overdoing things. But the truth was, I just couldn't get enough of the sport, because I'd become obsessed with not only it, but winning.

Things got to where I felt I could never tire out in the ring; that's how much I was training. I'd been told I was the "up and coming young boxer," and I was already dominating my weight class with a vengeance, even though I didn't have much competitive experience under my belt. Everyone around me had high hopes for me.

Nick leans in with a few last words of encouragement. "Remember your counterpunches. If he throws two, you throw two. You've got this." I roll my shoulders, fixated on Jay as Nick gives me a small push to move toward the center of the ring in order to bump fists. The ring is where I belong; it's where I live and breathe… where I feel alive. I bounce back to my corner, psyched up, anticipating the sound of the bell.

My opponent gives me an arrogant smirk, one that tells me he's gonna whoop my ass again, just like he has been for the past several fights. He's trying to psych me out; I know this, and I refuse to let it affect me. I grit my teeth in response, let out a low growl, and knock my gloved fists together, expelling some of my pent-up energy.

We both have well-defined physiques, narrow waists, and broad shoulders. We each also have a desire to win, but there's one major difference between us: I'm fearless. The more I'm hit, it only makes me want more, pushing myself beyond what is reasonable in order to overcome being defeated.

I start bouncing on my heels, ready to get on with the fight. At the sound of the bell, I don't even remember how I got to the middle of the ring. Adrenaline bursts through me as I throw the first punch, then immediately, I'm watching for the left cross. With Jay being a southpaw fighter, he's already got a huge advantage on the boxing world, but in a short amount of time, I've already come to understand his fighting rhythm.

I block him easily on the left cross then punch with an uppercut, while ducking my head to the left to avoid his counter again. He's left himself wide open, and I score a heavy hit to the side of his ribs.

I can hear people outside the ring shouting, but I'm too focused on the moment to make out what anyone is saying. I want to win just as much as I want my next breath, and before I know it, I'm starting to destroy him. It becomes more than obvious to me that he doesn't like getting hit the way he's been hitting me all along. Whether I'm able to dodge his punches or not is inconsequential. I've learned to come back with swift counterpunches, courtesy of Nick, matching him punch for punch. I'm relentless, unloading on him like never before, and I notice during this fight that he's shrinking back, time and time again.

Someone shouts from outside the ring, and it comes in loud and clear; it's Jay's dad, and he's not happy. I guess his father thought with Jay being a southpaw he'd be harder to beat in the ring, which is true. You don't see than many left-handers. Jay's dad, however, is a tyrant from Russia. He's a lot like my own father in some ways, a nice guy, an ex-fighter, and hard on his son, yet he's a gentleman.

By the end of the fifth round, both of us are getting exhausted from the grueling match. I sit down in my corner of the ring for a minute's rest, trying to catch my breath. Sweat drips from my brow but gets wiped away by a towel before it gets in my eyes.

Across the boxing ring, I look over at Jay to see his dad yelling at him until the man is red in the face. It's the same way my father yells at me, except I'm immune to it. Jay—not so much. I can tell his dad browbeating him is having the opposite effect. His dad is a nice enough guy, a real gentleman when he wants to be, but when it comes to the sport of boxing and his son, I've noticed he turns into an honest to

God tyrant.

I guess with his dad having been a pro-boxer at one time, he's been a real dictator to his son, pushing him to take his boxing career the distance. Even from twelve feet away, I can see the very second Jay's eyes go glassy, and my chest goes tight at the sight.

"Is something wrong with your chest?" Nick asks, concerned.

I shake myself out of my thoughts and look down, realizing I've been rubbing my upper chest with my gloved hand. And the tightness in my chest isn't from pain, but something else. It's an emotion I'm not used to feeling. I actually feel bad for this kid. I had no idea I'd been screwing with his confidence all this time, and it doesn't help that his father is adding to his humiliation.

I watch as his dad slams his fist down on the boxing floor, yelling something I can't make out, but I can see the continued effect his father's frustration is having on Jay. I don't like what I'm seeing, and even worse than that, I spy a lone tear that slides down Jay's cheek. The only reason I can see the tear is because it gives off a sparkle underneath the bright lights coming at us from the ceiling.

He then tries to hide his shame as if it were a bead of sweat, swiping at his cheek with the back of his red boxing glove.

"I don't want to fight him anymore," I blurt out without even thinking about it. I stay fixated on Jay as

I say this. His chest is heaving, and it's not from physical exertion. He's trying not to break down in front of everyone.

I seriously think I'm beginning to destroy more than his self-esteem in the ring, and I just can't be responsible for that.

A set of large hands come to rest on top of my shoulders. It's Nick. He massages my tight muscles while he leans down and whispers in my ear, "You're dominating a Junior Olympic winner already, with little competitive experience, Johnny. You can't give up now." There's a high level of pride and excitement to his voice, as he adds, "I've got really high hopes for you, kid."

I remove my gaze from Jay then twist around to face Nick, looking him square in the eyes. "No, I'm serious—I really don't want to fight him anymore," I tell him honestly.

"Why not?" Nick asks, taken aback and highly confused.

I shrug my shoulders, not really knowing how to convey my thoughts, let alone my emotions. "I just don't feel good about it." I jerk my chin toward Jay, and add, "Look at him. Can't you see what he's going through right now? I don't feel right about it."

Nick's eyes soften as he looks at me with something I can't quite describe. "You're gonna go far, kid... gonna go far."

Nick leaves my side and goes to have a talk with

Vic for a minute. When they're done talking, Vic then pulls Jay's father aside to have a few words. The fight's over. I forfeited the sparring match. I get up and leave the ring and head to the locker room to get my stuff. By the time I've cooled down and hit the outside streets, I'm feeling off. I'm starting to get a headache behind my eyes, a light pounding that holds promise of getting worse.

The cold sweat I've become all too familiar with radiates off my neck. *I just need to get home,* I think to myself, but that's my last thought as I fall headfirst into the busy city street and into oncoming traffic.

When I come to, I find myself lying down on the sidewalk and staring up into Nick's concerned face. I've never had a seizure hit me this hard before. I usually have time to get somewhere or put myself in a safe position before they hit. This time, I literally collapsed, having done a major face-plant into a busy street.

"My God, you scared the shit out of me," Nick says, looking into my eyes. "I need to call your dad to come get you."

"No," I croak, "I'll be fine." It doesn't matter how skilled you are, or how hard you train; if you aren't tough enough, you won't win. I have to be tougher than epilepsy.

Chapter 17

They fascinate me. I'm captivated by everything the racetracks bring and more. One of my favorite things to do at the track is to visit the race horses and pet them. I'm enamored by their majestic appeal. Each horse has their own shiny, rich coat of smooth, vibrant browns and blacks, and every shade in-between.

I love to see them do what they've been bred for. Even off the racetrack, they exude an immeasurable amount of stamina and power, and I can feel that very unspent energy rolling off them, especially when I run my hand over their massive, muscular bodies.

Out of all our gambling escapades, the racetrack is by far one of my most favorite places to be. There's just something about these high-spirited animals that keep me in awe. They hold such mystery, and a fiery blaze of passion lives behind their eyes. The way they shift on their feet before a race, their breathing growing heavier with each passing minute—they know exactly where they are, and really psyched up for the race. Adrenalized is more like it. They love to run as if the devil is on their tail while pushing their limits to run faster, harder, at high speeds, with the encouragement of the jockeys who ride them.

The dust kicks up from behind fifteen horses as they round the corner on the dirt track. From where I'm standing at the gate, I can hear their thunderous hooves hitting the ground as if they're in a stampede. This is going to be a close race. So many horses are neck and neck as they reach the final stretch, each horse pouring out their heart and soul, struggling to be the first to cross the finish line.

The roar of the crowd behind me is so loud it vibrates through my chest. My heart rate is jacked up, just like everyone else's, but mine's for an entirely different reason. I've got my own adrenaline rush going on. The commentator's voice blares from the outdoor speakers, getting louder and louder as the end of the race draws near, but I've tuned them all out. I have to stay focused and vigilant. Split second visuals is all I'm going to get; there are no instant replays, and there's no room for error.

I adjust the dial on my binoculars and zoom in as I follow the pack of horses in the final stretch. There's not a cloud in the sky, the sun beaming down on the tracks, giving me perfect visuals.

My left hand starts to shake from all the

excitement pumping through my body, so I steady my arm on the metal gate as I continue to follow the horses through the lens. I've paid close enough attention to who is who on the racetrack, so I already know everyone's number by heart. I have to. Most times, the numbers are hidden by other horses, and the fact they're all moving so fast means the numbers are merely a blur.

I watch with an eagle eye who the first three horses are as they hit the finish line. I couldn't hear the announcer by this point if I tried. I'm in my own zone, and I've got only seconds to play this game. I drop my binoculars, allowing the neck strap to catch their fall as I cup my hands over my mouth and shout as loud as I can to my brother, who's waiting on pins and needles for this valuable information. "Six, two, eight." I repeat the numbers one last time for good measure then watch with baited breath as my brother takes off in a full sprint, racing the clock. He runs from the fence line and then across the street to relay the information to Harry.

Harry is a good friend of my father's. He gambles with us quite often, including some of the back-alley card games. When he comes to visit us, he'd sometimes bring his daughter with him, who's a couple years older than me. God... the girl is smoking hot. Without a doubt, she has me infatuated with her.

I grab the binoculars from around my neck and look through them, not at the horses in their cool down run, but at my brother. I watch him as he shouts the numbers from a distance to Harry, who is already on the payphone with his bookmaker. He's placing his final bet with the winning numbers. This was a scheme of ours that required a full team effort, and we were extremely good at it.

There was no real-time reporting, and because of the lack of technology, we could call the bookmakers within seconds after the race, and of course, the bookies didn't know the race was already over. Some of the bookmakers weren't real sharp. My father kept a notebook of such bookies, and we'd use them to our advantage. It was a guaranteed win every time.

My father and Harry had a tried and true strategy. They'd bet on the second and third race after they'd just won the first race, but they'd purposely call in losing numbers. This was so the bookmakers wouldn't suspect foul play or catch on to their schemes. They'd do this with about five different bookmakers. Even though they didn't get caught, the bookmakers don't like to lose, and eventually they'd get cut off from betting with them again. The bookmaker's mentality is that they didn't want a "sharp" better.

One interesting thing to note about Harry, though —he's an active cop who lives in Queens, Ozone Park. He's a really good guy, but even he had a lesson to teach me early on. There's no loyalty when it comes to upholding the very laws he swore an oath to. I never really viewed him as corrupt, but New York did have their fair share of truly degenerate policemen.

Mixed messages lived all around me, day in and day out. There was a lack of a moral compass in a city that had not one direction to follow, but a matrix of chaos dipped in self-serving immoral acts of sin and crime.

~~*

I flush the urinal and make my way to the sinks to wash my hands when two big, burly men burst through the bathroom door, shoving a man forward as they enter. As the door closes behind them, I notice a couple security men standing just outside the door with their arms crossed.

I look around, noting the bathroom is half full; it typically is between horseraces. My eyes fall on the man who gets a fist to his jaw. His body first twists from the deadly blow just before he drops to the floor on his knees.

The two gangsters close in on the man, the look in their eyes telling me they're all business, and they're about to give this man a work over. The man on the floor surrenders, holding his hands out in a pleading fashion, but it does him no good. The time for talk is clearly over.

These are the type of men who don't care if everyone here is a witness to what they're about to do, and it doesn't take a genius to know they're not regular, everyday men. I knew they were gangsters at first glance, because I've been hanging around this type of environment since birth. I'm already hedging my own bets they're loan sharks.

"You think you're cute, don't you, Hank?" one of the gangsters asks. He calmly rolls up the cuffs of his blue dress shirt, getting ready for action.

"No—no," the man named Hank says, as if he should be believed. "I swear, I was going to have your money to you today."

The other gangster, who's wearing light-colored sunglasses, has heard enough. Like a flash of lightening, he strikes the man, delivering cold, hard blows with accuracy while yelling obscenities. Blood oozes from Hank's nose as he tries to block a few punches in vain. What baffles me is that the guy isn't even trying to fight back; he's just taking it—hit after hit. I guess he's thinking the less confrontational he is, the easier these guys will go on him, but he's thinking wrong.

Hank falls back onto the floor, holding his stomach and rolling around in pain as both men kick him with their highly polished black shoes, coming at him from all sides. He lets out an ungodly wail, crying out in agony.

All of the spectators including myself are watching, nobody moving an inch or lifting a finger to help the guy. Even security, who's right outside the door, knows what's going down in here, and they are doing nothing about it.

"You owe us money!" one of the gangsters yells.

"You have the nerve to show up here, playing with our money?"

Hank just continues to howl, not bothering to answer. There's nothing he could say at this point anyway. I'm so used to all the violence and bloodshed that watching people get beaten up doesn't affect me. In fact, I'm not sure there ever was a wow or fascination factor to begin with when witnessing such things as this.

I saw these types of beatings so often that, at this point in my life, I found myself more curious than anything as to how bad these gangsters would hurt the guy, or if Hank would fight back, which he hasn't. I'm constantly exposed to and watch wiseguys who keep getting screwed over by others, and then I become a witness to the fallout of what happens when said wiseguys are slighted or cheated. These people who borrow money from loan sharks, and then can't pay them back—I find it never ends well for them.

As I stand here watching these gangsters work Hank over, I catch my reflection in the mirror and look at my small build. I never want to be the victim like this man in front of me is, and I can't seem to grow fast enough or strong enough to get there. I know I'll wind up with my father's build, because I'm the spitting image of him in every way, down to how I walk. And it couldn't be any more evident of the pure Albanian blood that runs through my veins.

"Do you think I'm that stupid?" the gangster with

the glasses yells, and then spits on Hank. I whip my head to the side and look at the man who said those words. Looks can be deceiving, can't they? I can relate.

As my seventh grade teacher would say, *"I might look stupid, but I'm not."* I've found that to be my motto lately, and I might not be book smart either, but that's only because I really haven't cared to apply myself—but I am street smart. I've been told I'm far too perceptive for a kid my age, especially when it comes to numbers and assessing situations.

"Did you honestly think you wouldn't be recognized?!" Another kick to Hank's gut as the wiseguys use brutal force to get their point across. "That you could just come here and gamble our money away and not be seen?"

Hank cries out, "I'll pay it back! I promise!"

"Is that right?" one of the men mocks. "Boss is gonna want to know exactly how you're gonna do that." The distinct sound of fists and shoes hitting human flesh echoes off the bathroom walls.

Everybody here already knows it's pretty much impossible to be able to pay back a gambling debt. Who knows? The guy might have to get a second mortgage on his house if he hasn't already. If he has, then he's really screwed.

Hank coughs up a glob of red slobber then sputters with incoherent words. He looks as if he's about to pass out, too delirious to formulate a sentence anymore.

I can't help but wonder what this type of men would

do to my father if he got caught in these horse racing schemes of ours. It kind of hits home for me in this very moment as to just how dangerous this type of gambling is. I'm only a kid, but with the amount of time I spend in these places, like underground card games, the racetracks, or any other gambling situation my father takes me to, I realize my dad is fucking around with wiseguys and their income. He's beating them at their own games, and it's no joke.

If they ever caught us stepping in on their game, especially the way we've been manipulating some of the jockeys, it'll become a very serious situation. We were paying a certain number of jockeys we befriended, giving them a cut of the purse. They'd not only lose races, but they'd also collaborate with some of the other jockeys, blocking out some of the other horses to help cut out the odds. It was a win-win for everyone.

So, what we were doing wasn't as simple as trying to dodge a loan payment like this guy was. No, my father has surpassed the risky business, reaching a new plateau, taking his gambling to an entirely different level—a very dangerous level. High-risk stakes, the kind that would put our lives in jeopardy.

I'm pulled from my thoughts when the gangsters calmly walk to the bathroom sinks, wash their hands, and then straighten their jet black, greased hair, recomposing themselves. They turn and leave, not saying a word to anybody nor bothering to even glance back. With the show over, I make my way out of the bathroom just like everyone else, paying no attention to Hank, who's making low groaning noises.

"What took you so long?" my father asks when I finally meet up with him.

"I was watching a fight in the bathroom," I tell him. "Actually, it wasn't a fight. It was two gangsters who beat up another guy, because he owed them money."

My father shrugs it off. "Don't worry about it," he says passively, dismissing the conversation. "It happens every day."

I stop and think about that statement for a second, then say to myself, "Yeah... it actually does happen every day." It happens so much I didn't have to think twice about what to do. I knew enough to be quiet and to not inform the security guards, at which time they would've done nothing to help anyway. I also didn't go off running, trying to get help from my father or anyone else who I thought would save this man from getting beat up. Yes, this was an everyday occurrence in my life.

I guess I'm used to the madness growing up and surrounding me. I had always leaned on my father, trusting his every judgment and that he knew what he was doing. I thought he was being careful and he knew who or what type of wiseguy he was beating with their own games.

In the same breath, I also realize my father might be a fighter, but he's no killer, and he's definitely no gangster. So I can't help but think—what if that was him getting beat up in the bathroom? I suppose he'd deserve it in a way, because he's robbing them.

It's just odd to me that everything he's telling me not to do, we're doing. My father is always lecturing me, telling me not to screw with gangsters, not to do business with them or let alone steal from them. But everything in our lives is exactly that and everything between.

Every gambling event I went to always presented itself with a lesson to be learned. Even if some of them were repeated lessons, it only drove home its point like a sharp knife to the gut. There would always be one crazy incident after another at these affairs, and I was a witness to all of it.

I started recognizing early on this pattern of money management, or lack thereof. My father would talk about it, but he would never follow his own advice. He tried to budget himself, but gamblers can't. No matter what he would do in order to create a financial plan, he couldn't stick to it. Oddly, he made perfect sense when he talked about money and how to allocate it. So I paid close attention—very close attention.

Chapter 18

Times are changing on Jamaica Avenue, and the neighborhood I live in isn't happy about it. Already, there wasn't enough room for people to park their cars on the street on which we lived, so the city decided to make the residents pay for parking right in front of their homes. I guess the city needed to find another way to extort and make more money by installing parking meters up and down the streets and into our neighborhood.

Of course, not owning a car, this didn't concern me in the least. I didn't even think twice about it. As my friends and I were hanging out in front of a house, goofing off, talking about our day, and shooting the breeze as we normally do, we just happened to be hovering over one of these parking meters our neighbors despised. We didn't have any bad intentions; we were just playing around with it as we talked amongst ourselves.

I looked down and noticed the long pole extending into the ground was loose, and inevitably, as kids will do in testing the laws of physics and strength, two of my friends and I start pushing the meter back and forth just for the heck of it while we were talking and joking around.

"Hey! What ya doin?" a guy yells in a gruff voice at us from behind. All of us stop what we're doing and spin around to see a heavyset man standing behind his screen door. I'm not sure if he's pissed at us or not, and I think maybe we're about to get in trouble, because we've been messing around with the parking meter in front of his house.

"What ya doin'?" he asks again, as he opens the screen door to step outside and onto his front porch. The three of us exchange a quick glance at each other, none of us sure what his intentions are, so we remain quiet. His large gut protrudes from his wife-beater tank, testing the limits of the white cotton fabric. Waving his hand toward the three of us, adding, "With the meter?"

I don't know what to say to that either. My brows crease in confusion, and he must see the perplexed look I'm giving him from where he stands, so he elaborates.

"The meter—it's loose. What ya doin' with it?"

I'm still not sure if we're going to be in trouble for screwing around with the man's meter, because his gestures and tone are almost accusatory. He crosses his big, thick arms over his wide chest as he stands there thinking about something. I'm thinking, if he makes one more move toward us, we'll need to bolt, but instead, the strangest thing happens. He begins to chuckle then starts laughing, his large belly jiggling as he does so.

"You might as well keep playing with it till it's outta there," he says in his thick New York accent while wearing a broad smile.

Kevin and Charlie exchange an unspoken look with each other, all of us relieved he's not mad at us. The wheels start turning in my head, realizing this man wants us to get rid of the money draining problem, which has been nothing but a nuisance to the entire neighborhood since the day these parking meters were installed.

I look from the man on the front porch to the meter, giving it my full attention. I kind of feel like we've been given the task and the challenge to get rid of it for him. I look at Charlie and Kevin and give a shrug, my way of telling them we've got nothing to lose but time in which we were doing nothing important anyway.

So the three of us focus our attention on the meter, and grab onto it, pushing it back and forth. The old, gray haired man's laughter grows the harder we try to dislodge the pole from the cement.

"I didn't tell yous to do that, right?" he shouts in a jovial manner, making sure we all hear him.

I take pause and twist around, taking a good look at the man, and say, "All right." Kevin laughs at me, so I turn to face him with questioning eyes, and ask, "What?"

"You're the only one I know who can say, 'all right' or 'okay' in that froggy voice of yours and it mean so much more that what it's meant to." He shakes his head in wonderment and laughs at me.

The loose change clinks and jingles inside its casing and grows louder and more furious sounding the harder we shake the meter. There's nothing but dimes in the head of the meter, but it sounds full.

The three of us are working up a sweat, trying to loosen the metal pole from its concrete base, and the more violent and aggressive we get, rocking the meter back and forth, the louder the old man behind us laughs.

We're getting frustrated, because we've been working on it for almost an hour and it's hot outside. The pole is wobbly, but it's still not breaking loose. We refuse to give up, because we can feel it slowly giving way, and the cracking of concrete at our feet tells us so.

"Freaking finally!" Charlie hollers in elation as the base finally comes free, separating itself from the sidewalk. "I thought it'd never break loose."

All of us heave with all our strength and lift the meter out of its concrete hole.

"Good God!" Kevin huffs out. "This thing weighs

a ton."

Straining and pulling upward, everyone grunting and groaning from exertion, we're finally able to totally remove the meter. We lay it down on the sidewalk then stand up, trying to catch our breath.

I wipe the sweat from my brow and point at our handiwork, noting with winded pants, "Damn... I can't believe the hunk of cement stuck to its base. Must be at least fifteen inches in diameter. That sucker is heavy."

I look up the second I hear a set of hands clapping to see the old man applauding us while wearing a broad smile. I was so focused I'd forgotten he was still around.

"Now what? Where are we going to take it?" Kevin asks.

"My house is the closest," Charlie offers.

"All right," I agree. "Charlie, you take the meter end, Kevin takes the middle, and I will carry the cement end." We're going to need all the muscle we can muster for the two blocks it'll take for us to carry this monstrosity home. Kevin and I are the strongest. He's already breaching six feet in height, while Charlie —being on the heavy side—is the weakest of the three of us.

We each squat down, grabbing hold of our designated place on the meter's pole. Before we lift the heavy weight, I tell the other two, "On the count of three, we'll pick this beast up." They both confirm with a nod. "One… two… three."

We lift at the same time, Kevin making short guttural sounds as he struggles with the weight. "Don't poop yourself picking up the lighter end," I tease Kevin.

He starts laughing. "Don't make me lose it right now, jerkoff, or I'll wind up dropping this on my toes."

I try to contain my own laughter, as I ask him, "You good?"

"Yeah," he says in a strained voice. "Let's roll out."

None of us think twice about carrying the meter down the street for two blocks in broad daylight with a huge hunk of cement hanging off the end. No one says a word to us, or even gives us a funny glance, as we walk toward the park by where Charlie lives.

This is just another day with an anything goes mentality in Woodhaven. There's no need to be stealthy about it. None of us care anyway. By the time we're three-fourths of the way there, I think my arms are going to fall off. The cement end growing heavier and heavier with each step I take a fire ignites in my shoulders and biceps, but I ignore the burning sensation and push through the fatigue and pain.

Since Kevin is the one to go first when we reach Charlie's house, he winds up balancing the end of the meter on his thigh as he shoves open the front door.

We maneuver ourselves inside the foyer, and then start up the stairs. "This is gonna be tricky," Charlie quickly observes. He's not kidding; the hallways are narrow and the turns sharp. Everyone is grunting and groaning the entire way, because we're exhausted and we still have to heft this monstrosity, wielding it around at odd angles as we try not to put any dings in the walls.

We finally make it to his bedroom, and then carefully lay down what must've been a hundred pounds onto the wooden floor. We all collapse, taking a moment to recover as we study this *thing*.

"How we supposed to get the money out of it now?" Kevin asks.

"Hold on," Charlie says, snapping his fingers. "I got an idea." He gets up and leaves the room and is only gone a minute before he bursts back into his bedroom holding up a butter knife with a look of pride in his eyes.

He motions to the meter with his silver knife, and says, "Let's turn the meter over." So we roll it over so we can slip the butter knife into the coin slot. We start to jiggle the ten-ton weight, trying to create the right angle so the dimes can slide out over the flat surface of the knife. Dimes start to come out, one by one, and we get excited.

"Man, we hit the jackpot," Charlie says, his voice full of elation.

"Yeah we did," I respond with a smile. "There's a lot of money in here."

We're jiggling the hell out of this thing, and

quickly grow tired in the process. Things are moving way too slowly to keep holding this type of weight only to get a dime out here and there.

"Oh my God!" Kevin's voice gives way to frustration. "It's taking forever to get this money out!"

"Whatta yous doing in there?" Charlie's sister, Maureen, yells through the bedroom wall. Kevin and I roll our eyes. Maureen is a couple years older than us, but she's a real pain in the ass. "You're makin' a racket in there. I'm gonna tell Daddy," she warns.

"Shut up," Charlie bites back angrily. "Mind your own business."

We ignore her griping as we set the meter back down on the floor and re-strategize. "How about a drill?" I ask. "Does your dad have a drill?"

Charlie's eyes grow wide with the idea of what a drill can do for us, so he bolts out of his bedroom on yet another mission. He comes back, plugs the drill into the wall, and we set to work.

"Well, crap," Kevin utters, wrinkling his nose as he waves away the burning metal smell. With a haze of smoke in the air, and we all realize a tad too late we don't have the right drill bit. "We need a drill that can go through steel, not wood."

After another hour of hammering, beating, and re-drilling, we eventually get all the dimes out. We wind up splitting about sixty dollars between the three of us.

"I'm thinking the people who live on our streets

don't want these parking meters," I think aloud, as I bag up all my coins. I pause and look at my other two partners in crime, and ask, "What do you think?"

"I'm in," they both say at the same time.

"We need to figure out a better way to take these meters, though."

We all laugh exhaustedly.

~~*

We do wind up putting our heads together, and go in together on our first purchase—buying a pipe cutter. We find it takes mere seconds to cut the tops of the meter heads off, and we do it with great skill, leaving a barren meter pole behind.

And it's just as we thought—all the neighbors are backing us a hundred percent, wanting to get rid of the city's money-grubbing extortion just so residents can park cars in front of their own houses. It's as if we're doing them a favor, and I suppose we are in a way. So the message I got from not just one person, but from the entire neighborhood, was: *"It's okay to do something like this. We aren't hurting anybody. Besides, the city has plenty of money. As long as we don't steal from one individual, we aren't causing anyone any harm."*

In their minds, it benefits them too, because they don't have to pay for parking in front of their homes anymore. What's funnier is they'd even be on the lookout for us, coming out of their houses to help watch out for police. They didn't care we were doing this, so long as it saved them money and they didn't have to pay for parking any longer.

Once we learn this mindset of the neighborhood —and it doesn't take but a few more meters to see everyone is on our side—we're hitting every meter we can with a vengeance. Before we know it, we've got a system down-pat, running amok, only too happy to relieve the citizens of their burdens.

We never exchanged the loose change for dollar bills. It would've looked too suspicious. Instead, we'd go to the stores with bulging pockets full of quarters and dimes, counting the money out like a little kid who finally cracked open their piggy bank. And that's exactly what we'd tell the cashiers at the stores. They'd laugh with us and were even amazed of the nest-egg we had built up.

But there were only so many meters in our area, and all too quickly, we had exhausted our money trove. So we decided to start in on the next block available, including the ones on Jamaica Avenue. We'd always laugh passing by these headless meters, knowing that anyone who drove through town would see nothing but barren poles that once housed a meter head.

They stayed like that for a very long time. The city did nothing about it. Not even the police were called to investigate. There was no way to know if the meter collectors complained, but if they did, nothing was done to replace them. Of course, this was the city at its best in the early seventies. They were overworked, underpaid, and understaffed. Plus, they had bigger fish to fry than to chase meter thieves.

All the meter work was done boldly in broad daylight, with the exception of Jamaica Ave. We started taking those at night, and then we carried the meter heads home. And let me tell you, they were not light. We were dealing with forty pounds or so per meter, which, after walking with it for many blocks, became very fatiguing, but the payoff was great.

We even learned how to get into the meter heads with the proper drill bit. We grew highly proficient at this skill. But after we exhausted all the meters in our vicinity, that's when Charlie and Kevin bowed out, so I decided to expand on my own, not involving my friends.

I wind up enlisting some older kids to work with me, going up to the shopping mall. The Queens Center Mall, as a matter of fact, where the parking lot across the street housed four meters per pole. But this time, the deal became even sweeter. Each meter-head was housing quarters, not dimes. Because it's a big shopping center, the quarter meters would always be packed full.

We had to be extra fast to cut four heads off, because the parking lot was always busy, but it was big money. It only took a couple seconds to cut the heads off. Bing-bang-boom, and they were gone.

If I got four good meters, I'd get about $500 out of them. We'd take the meters back to my place and drill them in the garage, which was around the back of my house. Then I'd take the empty meters and toss them into the abandoned lot next to my house—the same place I previously tossed the keys to the elementary school.

After about six months, however, my little venture was becoming a little more dangerous. I'd already hit about forty percent of the meters in my town; I had to stop. There was no doubt in my mind by now I should've gotten caught and locked up. I'm sure the police wanted to target the meter thieves, since a large percentage had gone missing. Besides, the close calls were becoming more common.

It was the usual close calls, but nothing my friends and I couldn't handle. We never panicked and always played it cool. We had to; we knew there was going to be security and police cars circling around the mall at all hours, so one of us had to stay on guard, taking note of who was parked next to us and be super fast.

Again, even in the mall parking lot, as we'd take these meter heads, witnesses would see what was going on, but they didn't care. Their thought process was: *They're not bothering anybody*, and everybody we ran into appeared to have the same idea. It meant they didn't have to pay for parking. They figured, *It's only a meter. I don't want to pay or keep up with having to come back to add money to these meters—so let these guys take them.* It was also an era where people respected the fact it was none of their business.

I wound up doing all kinds of harmless yet criminal things growing up—but with each illicit thing I did, I was sent a mixed message every time, condoning the behavior. All our neighbors gave us the thumbs-up, supporting us. We weren't hurting anyone or stealing from individuals; we were hitting the city and its entity. The one that had all kinds of money to spare. As long as we were stealing from the city and were not bothering a "regular person" who worked hard for their money, then that was "okay" in their eyes.

Since then, so many other schemes and opportunities presented themselves to me, one after another, each one fully supported by not only my family, but the neighbors too. Even the policemen I knew weren't on the up and up. I had lost sight of right and wrong from an early age, because of one mixed message after another coming at me from every angle of life. As I got older, all the rights and wrongs of the world had merged into one, and in my head, I could justify anything.

Anything.

Chapter 19

"**Y**ou did what?" I scream at my mother, my hands shaking I'm so livid. I don't think I've ever been this pissed off at my mother or sister, not to this extent. "Do you have any fucking idea what you just did to me?" My voice peaks as pure rage consumes me.

I throw my fist into the living room wall, the same way my father has so many times before me. My mother, for the first time, actually looks afraid of me. Good. She just helped to fuck up my future, everything I've ever lived for. "I'm sorry," she says in a meek tone, which pisses me off more. There are not enough sorrys to make up for this one.

My mother had taken my sister to our family doctor yesterday, and my sister happened to open her mouth about me fighting and how I had a bad seizure, falling into the busy street. The doctor flipped out, not believing his ears. Then my mother filled him in on everything, down to my last boxing match and the seizure that happened right afterward. This doctor knew our family well, but not so well that he knew I was involved with boxing at the level I am. He's the one who has been prescribing my medicine for the epilepsy but remained completely unaware of my personal life.

Dr. Risoli stopped my Olympics match dead in its tracks just one week before my competition by calling the boxing association, alerting them to my medical condition. He did this, because he knew I had no intention of giving up this once in a lifetime opportunity, and I couldn't get another doctor to pass me on the physical. I was screwed.

My breaths are coming out short and heavy, unspent anger inside me, looking to find a way out. "Just so you know, I will never give up on boxing," I tell her with a mixed tone of determination and animosity. "I can't believe this," I snarl. Seething, I turn around and leave the house, slamming the door behind me as hard as I can, not giving a damn. I was only five days short of being able to fight without any hindrances or obstacles.

I can't get myself to cool off. There is no calming down. I've spent my entire childhood getting this far in the boxing circuit, only to get the rug yanked out from under me with one phone call.

I make my way outside and head down the neighborhood street, unsure where I'm going or what I'm doing. I'm just going. I wind up at one of my friends' house. A few of my friends are talking on the front porch, and they look every bit as angry as I feel. This gives me pause, not so much their mood, but for the fact they've each got a baseball bat in their hand as they talk amongst themselves.

"What's going on?" I ask as I approach.

One of them looks as if he could kill, and he's not that type of guy. These guys are the good ones; they're not street thugs and they don't get into trouble. They even go out of their way to avoid the 7N9 Gang.

"Father Farrill," someone says off to my side, utter contempt dripping from his voice.

"What about him?" I ask, confused.

"The bastard has been using religion to satisfy his sick fetishes," one of my friends tells me, "raping innocent boys." Nothing ever surprises me anymore, especially on the streets, but this news catches me off guard. "We're going to have our revenge," he adds.

The anger inside me coils in my gut, and I want to explode. "Let me help."

My friend shakes his head. "This is our battle, John."

"The brazen bastard fondled us every chance he got, and I have to hand it to him the way he did it, he was slick—very slick," another one of my friends says.

I feel sick to my stomach. I lean against the post of the front porch and look up at the overcast sky, not knowing how to digest this information.

"Some of the kids knew he took things further. Some of them didn't know. And some just knew something was wrong. I don't know what goes on in the mind of a kid when they get raped like that, or why they don't speak up," the oldest of our group tells me. "But you want to know the most sadistic crime of all? Besides this bastard Farrill raping these little boys for years in silence?"

I shake my head, and ask, "What?"

"The Catholic fucking Irish St. Thomas Church knew about it all this time and did absolutely nothing to stop it." My friend is seething like I've never seen before. A stormy rage brewing can be felt amongst them all. "They don't tell the police. They don't do anything. And you know why?"

I know the answer immediately. "Because they don't want it to come out."

"Exactly. He gets to ruin all these kids' lives without punishment. So we're about to deliver justice." The look in his eyes tells me he's going to be breaking bones today. "The motherfucker tried to kiss me once. I didn't understand it at the time, but I knew it was wrong, so I went off on him. I had no idea he had plans to take it much further."

"How did you figure this out?"

"He was at dinner with one of the families, when their little boy got out of his chair and went to hug him. Then the boy actually kissed him in the house, right in front of his own family! One thing led to another, and the truth finally came out. They called St. Thomas and told the clergy that this father is a rapist —a child molester—and those bastards already know, because they fumbled around with the news, wanting to sweep it under the rug."

"Let me help," I tell them again, nodding to one of their bats.

"No," he says firmly. "It's our battle. I know what times he's outside the rectory."

Hearing this news reminds me of the time when my father knew something was off with the priest but couldn't put a finger on it. Just like so many other people, I had respected him to a small degree, but that was because he wore a collar. I never really did buy into the "he's representing God" kind of thing. Truth be told, I thought the religion was kind of nuts, and that was because of my father and the fact he didn't believe in religion. My dad always viewed religion as a weakness.

My dad believed in a superior power, but he didn't believe in praying for things. He always thought that you were in charge of your own destiny, and we made things happen, not God. I was raised to rely on myself, that I make my own self strong, not God.

He wanted us to be soft in certain ways, but strong in others. An example of being soft would be if I went to the store with my friends, my father would tell me that if I could only afford one soda then not to buy it. He'd tell me to never go into a store and not treat my friend if he didn't have any money. And if he had no money, don't buy a drink in front him, or at least split one.

His thought process was to be soft with friends, but on the other hand, if anybody fucked me over, then to be tough with them.

Chapter 20

Silvana was small, petite, had a great smile, and her long, black hair complimented her piercing jet-black eyes in a way that could start a war among men. I loved her from the moment I laid eyes on her, which happened to be my junior year of high school. Going to school now held a new meaning for me. I suddenly cared, but not about my classes. I followed her around everywhere she went on a daily basis and slipped into as many classes of hers as I could just to sit beside her.

She was very school smart and worked after school most days in her father's fruit store. She came from an old fashioned Italian family, and she spoke her native language at home with precision. Silvana's parents sheltered her from the real world, so she wasn't jaded by life the way I was. She didn't have to contend with having to survive on the streets, be subjected to and a witness of acts of moral turpitude.

Her innocence was refreshing, and it was one of

the main things that drew me to her in the first place. She was sweet and kind, never having a bad thing to say about anyone. To put it mildly, there wasn't a mean bone in her body, and I soaked up every minute I could spend with her like a thirsty sponge.

I made all kinds of excuses so I could spend time with her after school, telling my family I needed to go to her house to get help with studying and that Silvana was willing to tutor me. I didn't care she lived a couple miles away. I found a way to get from Woodhaven to Middle Village, Queens without any problems.

She always had a core group of friends over at her house, and we had our own study group. They also were really good kids, and they never looked at me any differently because I was a rough street kid. They all accepted me into their fold without thinking twice. I felt like I belonged amongst them, and it was a nice break from all the violence and mayhem that inundated me day in and day out.

"Happy Birthday," Silvana whispers to me shyly, and then slips me a handmade birthday card in a hand-decorated envelope. Our fingers brush against each other's, and my heart skips a beat. Our relationship is a purely innocent one. She's like a fine porcelain doll to me, and I treat her as such.

"Thank you," I murmur in a low voice, my eyes softening as I meet her gaze. Her kind gesture hits something deep inside of me that's never really been touched before. Maybe that's because my family didn't celebrate my birthday.

My dad would say birthday cakes, cards, and the like were for sissies—for girls. My father never believed in birthdays; it just wasn't his style. But sometimes when he wasn't around, my mother would sneak me a cake and sing "Happy Birthday." I can't say it bothered me, because it was all I knew; it was my norm. My father made up for the lack of birthday wishes a thousand times over though, because he was a highly affectionate man, showing me much love on a consistent basis. He would hug and kiss all of us kids all the time and tell us that he loved us.

Silvana was always unselfish and full of thoughtfulness. I smile as she opens a brown paper bag then reaches inside to pull out a cupcake with vanilla icing wrapped in cellophane.

"You going to sing to me too?" I tease with a lighthearted grin. I know she will. She has a beautiful voice and loves to sing to me.

"Of course I am," she says in her lyrical way, her beautiful smile on full display.

I smile fondly at her then take the card and cupcake, setting it on the desk in front of me. As I start to open my card, someone calls my name from the front of the classroom. I look up to see the teacher, Ms. Loeb, standing by the pencil sharpener attached to the wall, and she's doesn't look so happy. The look on her face is stern as she uses her index finger to beckon me from my seat. I put the card down and get up then follow her outside the classroom and into the hall so she can speak to me privately.

As soon as she shuts the classroom door behind her, she turns to face me. "You don't belong in this classroom, Johnny," she begins. "You need to go to your own class."

"I'm not going anywhere." I shake my head in defiance and point my finger at the shut door to where Silvana's sitting. "I love that girl in there," I tell Ms. Loeb with serious conviction.

She pauses for a second, and I watch her face as she digests my words. She realizes just from the tone of my voice I'm not going to budge and she's not going to change my mind. She's fully aware I'm a big baseball player, popular in school, but she also knows I'm not the greatest of students.

Ms. Loeb studies me for a moment, seemingly trying to hide a grin.

"Okay," she says slowly, "you can stay if you type."

The tension in my shoulders immediately goes slack, and I breathe a sigh of relief on the inside. "I can do that," I assure her, accepting the challenge with a grin. I would do anything—anything at all—to keep my school crush near me at every turn.

She nods her head in agreement. "All right, I'll work out the class change with the principal, but you'll be held to do your part," she says sternly, not about to give me any leeway as she points a finger at me.

I hold out my hands. "Not a problem," I tell her. "I'll be your best student."

She grins at me and shakes her head, and it's then I know she's a hopeless romantic. She also knows I'll do well in this class, so it's a win-win for everyone, and Ms. Loeb will feel as if she's contributed to the betterment of my education. We shake hands and close the deal, both of us smiling.

I go back into the classroom and take my seat next to Silvana, who's silently questioning me with those beautiful, dark, piercing eyes of hers. I just give her a wink, lean in, and tell her, "It's all good. I'm your new typing partner."

~~*

The doctors said I'd grow out of it, and for the most part I did, but I could still feel them coming on. I had become very in tune with my body by the age of sixteen, so I could tell when a seizure was about to happen. I was able to recognize the warning signs and then prepare myself.

I couldn't stand the medicine the doctor put me on, which was Dilantin, the only drug of choice. The drug messed with my mouth too much, made my gums swell, and it was very painful. Even though it was a great drug for epilepsy, I hated being dependent on anything other than myself, so I took control of my own health and quit the meds. It was probably the wrong thing for me to do, but I was too headstrong for anyone to change my mind.

I was careful to manage all the different things that sparked these seizures, but sometimes the stress, lack of sleep, fights, and getting knocked in the head would eventually catch up to me, and I'd finally have an epileptic episode. These seizures would leave me depleted of energy for the entire day, and all I could do was lie in bed and sleep off the exhaustion.

I thought giving boxing a rest for a couple years would've been enough, would've given my body time to heal from epilepsy, but I was wrong. When I went back to the sport at sixteen, all of my seizures sparked up again, and worse than before. Everyone around me was warning me to stop boxing, and sadly, I could see the writing on the wall, so I gave it up again for the second time, which has really messed with my head. I love boxing, and it cut out a piece of my soul each time I had to quit.

There was nothing left for me at this point but to try to go pro with baseball. So that's where I've been applying all my time, efforts, and energies. Baseball has now become my entire existence, my number one focus for trying to escape the streets.

I don't know if it's a natural chameleon thing I was born with, a subconscious skill of survival, or if I just knew I had to beat the streets and become the most charismatic person in order to blend in and get along with every gang, mob, and every other group within New York City boroughs. Maybe it was a combination of the three. Either way, I was fortunate to have friends on all sides, in every facet of life, and that wasn't an easy feat to accomplish.

I had the skill to adjust, and it became so natural to me on a subconscious level I didn't even recognize when I was transitioning my personality, fitting in with and communicating on other people's levels, from regular kids, street kids, adults, gangsters, corrupt police officers, and gang members. My friends and family were the ones to point it out to me, commenting I could switch gears in the blink of an eye with the way I acted, walked, talked, and behaved.

I can look like a proficient gambler, an up-and-coming gangster, a talented boxer, or a skilled baseball player with a promising scholarship, and then I can turn around and give the appearance of a tough-guy on the street, who projected someone to be feared, where one would think twice before messing with me.

Whether I liked it or not, I was immersed in all these facets of multidimensional lifestyles and cultures, weaving in and amongst them with ease. With me being involved with a countless number of people from so many diverse backgrounds, it gave me status, and I was granted privileges, able to go into certain neighborhoods and areas within the city that most would never dare venture into.

So before I knew it, I was covered all the way across the board, not having the amount of stress that the rest of these kids had. Everyone was highly aware of my contacts from all walks of life, which made me popular with the other kids. Many used me as a shelter, wanting to hang out with me or go places with me, because they couldn't handle the racial tensions and all the violence going on around them.

Because I was still having to survive in the day-to-day life in which I was still living—I know I've already become part of the streets—involved in too many things to ever truly be able to back out of it entirely. The streets spared no one, and it was a ruthless and vicious place to be.

I never did get to experience a true childhood. I had to grow up too quickly. So at the age of sixteen, I already knew from my own gambling experiences and street smarts that I had to diversify my skills. I already had hundreds of schemes going on at the same time, and it was a lesson I learned when my boxing career fell through. The forfeiture just cemented what I'd known all along, becoming painfully obvious. I had to branch out.

Chapter 21

I slip my T-shirt back on, having just shown some of the 7N9 Gang members the finished tattoo I recently got on my back.

My grandma, my grandfather's sister, and my mom's sister were the ones who encouraged me to get the Albanian flag along with Skanderbeg, the hero of the Albanians, so I did. This actually made both my grandfather and dad very proud. It wasn't hard to afford. I have a newspaper route, and I work at the deli, plus I hustle anything I can get my hands on in order to make money. I always have my hands on money, but I seem to spend it just as fast as I can make it.

"Very cool, man," Steven says with admiration in his voice. I turn around, straightening out my shirt, and grin.

"Thanks." Despite the few skirmishes my brother and I have had with some of the members, all of us keep a mutual respect for one another and still hang out on occasion.

My friend Mike comes bursting through the front door of his house, stepping out onto the front porch where me and a bunch of the 7N9 members have been hanging out for the past hour just killing time. The look on Mike's face tells me everything I need to know.

"Riot at Thomas Edison," he announces to everyone in a deep voice full of tension. "Just got a phone call from Timmy."

Timmy is obviously one of their own, but he's also a good friend of mine. The thing is, he goes to high school with my brother, who is also caught up in the violent mix, and it's all because of racial tension.

"Sounds like it won't take much to get out of control," Mike adds in a serious tone. We all know the drill. This is where having numerous friends with power and pull has benefits. In times such as these, we all pull together to get our own kind out of the violent chaos.

My high school, Franklin K. Lane, had shut their doors for about four years, because nobody could get a grip on the violence, drugs, and everything between. When Franklin High opened their doors again, I just happened to be entering ninth grade and I was slotted to go there, but my brother and everyone else from our neighborhood were already established at Edison High School in Jamaica, Queens, and they weren't allowed back in their very own school district.

Not that my brother or anyone else wanted to go to Franklin K. Lane either, because it was just as bad. The city was busing in lower income communities from all black neighborhoods who didn't live in our school district, which was an all white neighborhood, and it didn't go over very well.

These kids being transported here were much older than us, because they were held back academically two or three times. The school was filled with nineteen and twenty-year-olds, half of them with beards. It was the exact scene in my junior high too.

These kids were held back either because they didn't go to school, they started a year or two late from kindergarten, or they were academically held back. Those who should've been in ninth grade were still in sixth or seventh grade, and this was the majority of these kids coming in. The parents' outcries fell on deaf ears.

The problem where Edison High was concerned, it was housed in the heart of an all black neighborhood, and race riots were at an all-time high. We were fighting against everyone, from small gangs to well established gangs like the Black Panthers.

What many people outside of the city didn't realize, is most of the fighting that was going on wasn't so much with the kids who were attending school; it was the gang-related kids hanging out around the schools who would attack.

These gangs and street kids who helped instigate

the riots lived for violence like this—they thrived off it. They just wanted to fight to fight and to hurt people. There was no rhyme or reason to the violence. It was just pure insanity.

The white kids would attack the black kids who passed through our neighborhood or went to school in my district, and the black kids would attack the white kids who were attending school in their district. It was a never-ending vicious cycle.

For the white kids from our neighborhood, they would be trying to reach the J train unscathed so they could get home. It was an eight-block walk of pure hell through all black neighborhoods, and it was a hundred times worse if there was a riot breaking out.

Me and my friends were always running over to the high school when the race riots boiled up, helping to retrieve all the kids from our own neighborhood to get them home safely. It was damn near a daily ordeal. Someone was always calling from the school, trying to get a hold of one of us guys in Woodhaven to spread the word to get a group of our own guys together, so we could run over there and help them.

"We need to hurry it up," Steve says, getting to his feet, the urgency in his voice evident of the critical situation.

"How many we got?" Mike asks him.

"We have ten guys that are ready to go," he replies.

Without hesitation, we all get up, gathering weapons from Mike's stash before taking off. As we each gather extra knives or black jacks, Mike is making a few more phone calls to gather more gang members, and we need to get there before one of our friends gets hurt real bad, or worse, killed.

Sometimes, we'd go fight with about twenty guys, some of us going in cars, others jumping on the J train, trying to get there as fast as possible. We knew what we were up against, and each our fighters counted, as we knew we'd be fighting not only bigger guys, but sometimes over thirty members of another gang.

I never thought there'd come a day when I'd actually be part of a historical movement in time— and of course, it wasn't apparent at the time we were going through it. But all of these race riots were a pivotal point in American history, and I was right in the middle of it, fighting right alongside my friends.

~~*

We're all running, rushing through the neighborhoods, needing to get to my brother's high school for what's about to go down, if it hasn't already. What can start out as six kids fighting can quickly morph into fifty out of control, and these gangs don't come out to play. They come out to maim, hurt, and kill.

The older I got, the more things in my life suddenly took a turn for the more serious. I knew early on death was always lurking around the corner, but I wasn't going to let it take me—not without a major fight first. So if I wanted to survive in this type of life, I knew I had to take everything to the next level. If someone brought a knife to a fight, I had to bring a bigger knife. If there was a gun, I made sure to have two, and I wasn't fucking around anymore. I'd seen enough, been part of enough, and I meant business, because I wasn't going to be the victim. I was going to do everything within my power and abilities to prevent that from ever happening, and that meant I had to be preemptive.

Half of the 7N9 Gang members cram into Mike's car while the other half of us make our way toward the J train. As the eight of us round the corner, we almost bowl over a handful of young girls skipping rope, doing what's called double-dutch jump roping. These girls have no idea what's truly going on around them, or maybe they do. Because the sound of about thirty feet slapping the pavement at a runner's pace, with the majority of the guys wearing their gang colors and holding bats and other weapons, can't be missed. Most of the girls aren't even curious or bother to look our way.

Just as the gang and I round the next block, we're all witnesses to a beat-up car rolling up to one of the houses to our right, and within seconds, gunfire erupts from the car's windows. The sound of glass shattering from the house's windows can barely be heard over the weapons being discharged from the vehicle. Shot after shot rings out in multiple succession. The car tires screech as the driver hits the gas to peel away, leaving just as quickly as they came barreling in.

The Norman Rockwell scene I previously saw only a block before was a farce. There is no escape from this life; it's just fucking violent insanity everywhere I turn.

"Can you believe that shit?" Steve huffs out, breathing heavily from our run.

"Yeah, man," I tell him. "If we would've cut down the other block, we would've been right in the line of fire."

Neither of us needs to say anything more. Things like this have been such a common occurrence for decades. It's no big deal to either be a witness to it or have an untold amount of close calls.

We leave the scene behind, just like the car, unconcerned for anything except the mission we're on. I'm used to running miles; that's never changed for me. It's an adrenaline rush for me to stay in optimum shape for baseball, but some of these gang members who are doing drugs and not exercising are expending much of their needed energy on this run to catch the train.

By the time we do hit the J train and jump on, some of the guys are holding their sides, out of breath from the sprint to get here.

I look at Steve, who appears to have caught his breath rather quickly, as one of the gang members asks him, "What'd Mike say?"

"Someone sucker punched Timmy earlier today, and it didn't go well for the other guy."

And this was what would usually spark a riot—a plain and simple fistfight—and nothing more than that. Everyday fights just like this one that went on inside the school. Then it carries out from there, the other guy telling his friends so he can get backup, sometimes having thirty or more guys waiting to jump one kid. And this time, they're wanting to jump Timmy.

The majority of the fights weren't like a last-second thing. We'd know when a riot was planning on breaking out days ahead of time. The school did too, because many of the kids who caught wind of the upcoming fights were scared, and they'd go tell the teachers and principal. Sometimes the threat of an all-out war would be so bad the school would either bring on extra cops or close the schools down for days at a time.

All the kids would be fighting, and no one wanted to go to school, because of the riots going on outside. Every kid was worried about getting stabbed or beat up, and many would try to hide weapons on their body. Even if there were metal detectors, most of us knew how to beat them. We had security guards that were friends of ours, and they'd help us pass through.

Besides, these guards couldn't grab every single kid who was carrying something, even during a shakedown.

The black kids were known to keep razors in their mouths or in their afros. They were afraid, just as afraid as the next kid.

"You know how it goes," Steve says, making small talk with me. "When you have a couple bad kids that are prejudiced, you can't talk to or make friends with the black kids, or you fight with the white kids, and vice versa."

"Yeah—I do know how it goes," I tell him. "It was that way in grammar school too, but it wasn't as bad as it is now."

"All right, guys," Steve says to his friends as the train stops, "let's go!"

We must be a real sight, a group of guys in gang colors holding weapons while everyone's wearing looks that could kill. All of us jump from the train and take off at a run in the direction of the school.

By the time we make it to the scene, Mike and his group of guys are just piling out of his car. And this is when a gang like 7N9 is good to be friends with. Because when the kids from our neighborhood call home needing backup, the gang pulls together.

Glancing around the schoolyard, it's obvious what started out as a small fight of maybe six or seven has turned into thirty, because just as we're coming on the scene, so is the other side. They come at us wielding chains and bats, and I'm thinking in this moment of what my father has taught me.

He told me there would be times to be afraid where I was going, but to just fight, because that fear will go away once I start fighting. And it always held true.

I know everybody else is just as scared; the only difference is the other kids didn't have the training my brother and I did. Because Timmy Donahue hung out with us often, my father taught him a lot of moves. He was a tough guy in his own right, and he'd fight just like us. One thing I could say with certainty about the Irish—and this Irish gang—is they will fight. Even if an Irish guy can't fight, he won't back down. The Fighting Irish is a good name for them all.

I glance around and spot my brother, Timmy, and Joe Galliano along with a few more of their friends in the heat of battle. I rush at the first guy I see, who's going after my brother from behind. He's wearing his own set of gang colors on his jean jacket. He catches sight of me rushing him, so he rears his arm back and then swings his fist my way. All I can see is a big curled hand coming at me, cold-cocking me square in the jaw. Everything blurs for a second, but it doesn't stop me. It's as if my body is on autopilot, all the muscle memory I have for counter moves happens without me even thinking about it.

Out of the corner of my eye, I catch a flash of silver catching the sunlight, forewarning me that a set of heavy chains are about to take me down. I duck out of the way but am left open to several more punches from the guy I'm fighting. I know it's a matter of seconds before those chains are going to come back at me, and I'm not sure I'll be so lucky the second go around. The guy with the chains doesn't see Joe Galliano coming in from the side. It only takes a few good punches to the guy's head, and then he goes down, Joe having knocked him out.

When I turn around to look for the next guy to fight, I catch sight of my brother, who's been getting hit by a baseball bat all along. His face is already a bloody mess. Fury bubbles up out of me. I'm almost to my brother to help take this guy down when I hear the bat make connection with his fist, and instantly, I know he's got a broken hand. But his adrenaline is so high it doesn't faze him. He's still fighting with everything he has.

I come in from the guy's side and start laying into his ribs like a punching bag. Mass chaos is everywhere, but this isn't anything compared to what I've seen before. Sometimes these gangs would come in such force and get so out of control they would turn over buses and police cars, busting out their windows.

All the schools, such as this one, have cops on duty, but there isn't enough of them. So everybody gets in at least ten to fifteen minutes of hard fighting before they get busted up.

No sooner do I get the bat from the guy who

unleashed on my brother, I hear police sirens in the distance. Some people keep fighting; others start to retreat and split up.

By the time the gang I'm with regroups, making sure we've got all the people we came here for, we take off. I look back over my shoulder and see an ambulance and cops swarming all over the schoolyard. Other kids are still running, some not getting away in time and are now being arrested.

With certainty, none of us from either side of the fight had called the police. It's everybody else who's freaking out. Usually, it was the schoolteachers, or the cops stationed at the school who called for backup. It just wasn't in our mentality to call the cops.

Our group clamors onto the J train to head back home, everybody beaten and bloodied up. We were used to getting into fights more severe than this one, so it isn't even on our minds that anyone should go to the hospital. Nobody from our crew ran to hospitals in pain.

The train jerks forward as we take off, and then I look at my brother, and ask, "How you doing?"

"I'm fine," he says without emotion, but he's cradling his injured hand.

"We need to stop at the doctor's and get a cast on that," I tell him.

He just nods his head in acknowledgement.

"Fuck," Timmy groans from the next seat over, turning my attention to him. He removes his hand from the side of his head to see his palm covered in bright red blood. He's got a nasty gash to the side of his head, and there's no doubt he's going to need a dozen stitches. I quickly take off my T-shirt then roll it up to press it against his head to help stop the bleeding.

"Man, you look like shit." I make the comment as I stare at his bloodied face.

"Shut the fuck up," he growls back, and then we both laugh at each other. I know now he'll be fine. It's Timmy, and he's tough.

Nobody contacted their parents; otherwise, we'd be calling our parents every day for fights like these. But the parents were either oblivious to the hell we were going through, or they couldn't wrap their heads around what was truly going on around us and just how dangerous these riots were. It's not like kids aren't getting stabbed... and it's not like kids aren't getting killed. All of this was going on.

We were on our own, and believe it or not, this was the same shit that happened to us in junior high. All of the race riots, you had to be tough and on guard, and ready to fight at any time.

"What happened?" I ask Timmy.

"Some ass sucker punched me. So when I started fighting him, another guy jumped on him, and then your brother jumped in," he explains, but pauses to spit out a mouthful of blood first. "And I knew shit was going to hit the fan after school."

"Yeah," I say, "looked like it went from seven or eight guys to thirty within seconds."

"Before I knew it, guys were getting cracked over the head with bats, pipes, sticks, and chains, all because of one little fucker who felt he needed to sucker punch me."

"I think a lot of it is about who gets to be in the stronger position—the one who gets to be in control over everybody else."

He nods his head, but I hold it still with my other hand as I apply more pressure to the side of his head. He closes his eyes for a minute, letting me help him, then murmurs, "This is a hell of a way to go to school, isn't it?"

"It's an endless cycle," I muse. We understand the level of violence we're dealing with, and even those who usually *want* to go to school, don't want to go because of the violence. A lot of nice kids got caught up in the middle of these wars, but they're stuck if they want an education.

~~*

We weren't living in a boxing ring. This was real life, and the consequences were permanent. My Father didn't understand this. Even though he was a fighter, he was one who believed in rules. But there were no rules on the street.

Chapter 22

Too many transitions are happening all around me, and all at the same time, which in all actuality has been this way my entire life. But this time, I feel as if I've reached a pinnacle. I've been making more and more of my own decisions about my future, and I'm cognizant of the fact I might not be making the best of choices.

Maybe it's years and years of suppressing my emotions and all the repressed anger that has been bottled up for far too long. Because I feel something deep inside of me has been at a slow boil for a while. Things like me never making it to the Junior Olympics, losing an abnormal amount of friends and family members along the way, some who never even got to see their prom.

The mob exposure, violence, race riots, gangs, and gambling schemes have taken a toll on me as well. The only thing I feel I have going for me is a possible

baseball scholarship, but as I learned early on—
nothing is guaranteed in this life.

I can't totally rely on baseball alone as my only way
out. I'm not sure about anything anymore, and I know
better than my father does when it comes to money
management. It's not as easy as everybody thinks it is.
Although going pro is what I want, the reality is I
need a backup plan in order to make money. It's very
forward thinking for a sixteen-year-old boy, but I grew
up fast. I had to.

I had to start hedging my bets, so to speak.
Diversify by not putting all my eggs in one basket,
especially when it comes to ensuring the success of
my future.

I've been working at Dick's Deli on Jamaica
Avenue and 79th Street for a couple years now. Funny
thing how gambling and gangsters are always in the
forefront of my life. I came to work at a deli and
wound up working for gangsters on the side, all the
while being clocked in at the deli. My boss was a
gambler too and didn't have a problem with me
working for them as well.

It all started out innocently enough. Etor was a
guy who hung out at the deli, and he was constantly
using the payphone in the back of the deli to conduct
the majority of his business. He was running numbers
and sports bets from the deli for a wiseguy named
George Caddy, who was from the Lucchese family.

I became a major convenience for the crew,

because as Etor would take bets, he'd write the names and betting amounts on a paper slip then hand them to me to run them across the street to turn in to George.

At the end of each week, he'd throw me a small percentage of the money they made just for running bookie slips for him. It was BS money, but at least they were paying me.

A little later on, as technology was improving, Etor attached a recording device to the telephone system at the deli. This allowed him to record every conversation so nobody could cry foul play, trying to manipulate the system if they lost a bet. Obviously, it wasn't a good thing if the cops ever got a hold of this device, but they had a failsafe system they would implement if the cops happened to bust in. They used a heat-triggered recording device that would self-destruct when the user sent a signal, causing a coil to heat up within the unit, which would then dissolve the device within seconds.

~~*

The 7N9 Gang was always hanging out on the corner near the deli where I worked. Everyone was gambling, getting high, and drinking there, including the workers. All the while, the bookmakers were in the back, making deals at all hours of the day. This was the type of work ethic I was exposed to, so it was inevitable I was going to get exposed to more and more trouble.

I'm working the deli today and cleaning up from the afternoon rush, when I hear a lot of commotion on the corner, and then I see a few people running down the street. My brows furrow in question as curiosity gets the better of me, and I head toward the exit. The bells chime above my head as I open the door, a cold blast of crisp fall air hits me as I step out onto the sidewalk, but I feel nothing. I'm too focused on all the commotion.

"What the hell?" I murmur, as cops swarm the corner, flashing blue lights everywhere. I don't even realize I'm walking toward the chaotic scene until I'm standing beside many of the 7N9 Gang members.

What I see next stops me in my tracks. A Spanish kid is in a contorted position, half his body on the street, and the other on the sidewalk, as he lies in a red puddle of his own blood. His jacket is unzipped, revealing a blood-soaked shirt.

His eyes are open, glazed over actually, and it's obvious he's not breathing. He's dead. Stabbed to death. Just before a special blanket gets placed over his entire body to hide the horrific scene from the public's eye, I catch sight of Michael's knife as it lies on the sidewalk beside the lifeless body.

I'm no stranger to being a witness to death or extreme violence. I'm unaffected by it—just the same as these gang members—but what we're not used to is seeing one of our friends having taken a fight to the next level, experiencing a murder firsthand.

Michael Stratton wasn't a close friend, but he was still a friend. Even if one wasn't officially in the 7N9 Gang, me and a lot of other non-gang members all hung out on this corner with them. Michael, Kevin and Steve Bonner, George Catalano, Joe Galliano, Timmy Donahue, and me have known each other since we were kids. Everyone knew everyone.

A policeman places his hand on top of Michael's head, guiding him into the back of the police cruiser. His wrists are cuffed behind his back, and he's painted in blood. The car door slams shut, trapping him inside, and my gut sinks. Scanning the corner, I can't process the scene fast enough.

Richie, one of the gang members, and a friend since junior high, comes over to me with a solemn look on his face. Everyone is silent. Stunned might be a better word to describe everyone's demeanor.

"It was plain and simple," Richie tells me in a low voice, informing me of what just happened. "It was a fight that Mike was willing to take to the next level. The Spanish kid misjudged just how serious Mike would get, and he paid for it with his life." He pauses, taking a long drag off his cigarette. When he exhales, he watches the smoke curl in the cool air above, as if he's reflecting back on the scene. He shakes his head as if waking from a thought then looks at me. "That's it—plain and simple."

In the back of my mind, I realize as I'm standing here, the next time violence plays out, it could be me who's the victim. I could be the next one to be killed, stabbed like this kid was, and lying in my own pool of blood.

We were all kids, but we were turning into young adults, and moving into new levels of crime. What just happened here on the streets today—one can't go higher than this. Taking lives, and then going to prison for it. It's serious shit.

It's all very sobering… eye-opening to many of us standing around the crime scene. Nobody said it. We didn't need to. We all knew we were becoming killers. Not just petty criminals or smalltime drug dealers anymore… but dangerous, cold-blooded killers.

I'm moving into new territory whether I like it or not, and even though I'm not directly involved with *today's* situation, I am very much *involved*. I am affected by all these bad experiences, and with each day that goes by, they're all adding up, hand over fist, making me rethink my future—my survival.

Vulnerability has hung in the balance my entire life, and I can't allow myself to ever be the victim. And before people and circumstances take control of me, I need to take control of them.

I was just a kid who was always hustling for a quick buck, but now I'm deciding it's time to step up my game. It's time for me to pass everyone and take charge.

It's about business, power, and money now. That's the bottom line. And I'm the only one who has the nerve and guts to take action. I know I'm ready, and I know I'm very capable. And it's not to make the move to get into drugs. It's taking all the necessary steps in order to "take over the neighborhood." In other words, I've got to let everybody know that I'm *the guy* now. The one in charge—the one to be feared.

I can feel the future. I never denied it. I want to go to that level. I'm enamored by it. I'm taken in by the power of money and the possible wealth I could obtain from free enterprise—legal or not. Including in my mind if I had to kill somebody, I would do it.

It was a path of destruction no one saw coming, and it'd be full of violent deaths.

Chapter 23

I just happen to look up and out the deli's front window at the exact moment a black kid is going by on his bicycle and minding his own business. He's suddenly knocked off his bike as some gang members jump him then start beating the hell out of him. Sadly, I've even seen people go so far as to run other kids over with their car and drag them down the street.

There's really only a handful of bad kids doing these bad things, but it's enough, and I hate it. I have friends from every race, color, and creed imaginable. So I'm not really sure it's hatred toward a specific race. Sometimes, I think it's just a hatred of life in general and the way we're all being raised. Many of us live in poverty, and we're being piled in on top of one another in an overcrowded city, so naturally, bad things are bound to happen.

In saying this, racial tensions are still at an all-time high, and nobody is controlling anything. White people are treated the exact same way in the black neighborhoods as the black people are treated in ours.

Everybody from all sides know their boundaries, and they know what risks are involved if they happened to trespass into the wrong area, especially at night.

Part of being stuck in some of the wrong neighborhoods could be anything from having just attended a baseball game or school letting out, and then knowing we have to get out of the area before it started to turn dark. It was just something all of us knew we had to do; otherwise, we'd be signing our own death warrant if we stayed or happened to venture into the wrong area at the wrong time.

The majority of both black and white kids were typically good kids. It wasn't like everybody was stereotyped to be bad, whether they were white, black, Hispanic, or other. But we had to pay attention and respect boundaries, or risk consequences. Whether anyone liked it or not, it's just the way things were.

Everyone's ignoring the beaten kid out on the street—yet another all too common scene. My attention is pulled from what's going on outside as someone taps me on the shoulder. I shift my gaze to one of the regulars. He's always in here, and he's typically high.

"Have you seen Tommy?"

I shake my head.

"Well, do you know where I could get a fourth from?" he asks, hopeful.

"No, man, but if I see him, I'll let him know you were looking for him."

He thinks about that for a moment, then asks me, "How late you working to?"

I glance behind me and look at the dingy clock on the wall. "About five more hours."

He gives a quick nod, coming to terms with something in his head, then reaches into the front of his jeans to pull out a wad of cash. He slips it to me, and says, "I've gotta go somewhere, but I'll be back in a couple hours. Let Tommy know you can hold my stash, and I'll get it from you when I come back." He pauses, then leans in to add, "There's thirty bucks extra in there. That's yours."

"Yeah, sure," I tell him. "Not a problem."

He smiles, happy he doesn't have to sit around and wait for Tommy, and without phones being easily accessible, there's no way to get ahold of him to see when he's going to show up.

So this is how the drug business started for me, all because everyone has known me for years on end, and I'm just as familiar and friendly with them.

The deli is supposed to be a job to do the right thing after school—but it turned into the wrong thing because of the environment. I fell into it innocently enough. It's not like people approached me and asked if I could exchange drugs or money for them. I fell into it the same way I did with the bookmaker.

I became a convenient go-between for everybody, because I was always here working, and before I knew it, I was exchanging both monies and drugs.

The venture becomes more and more of a steady thing. It's as if I get enlisted for the job without signing on the dotted line. I become trustworthy to everyone around me, which makes me more and more popular.

I make quite a bit of money from playing the middleman. On occasion, I make as much as $500 a week, but the commissions aren't so much that I think I can get into this business on my own. However, the longer I do this, the more opportunities arise.

Joe Galliano has known my brother and me for a really long time. He played baseball with us, and had a lot of talent, just like my brother. He's been dating my sister for some time now and happens to be one of the dealers working through the deli, selling drugs.

We were talking one day, and he was telling me he was having some problems with Albert Ruggiano, whose father was the boss in our area. Albert wanted a percentage of the business attacks. That's what they would call it; either that, or they'd call it a shakedown. Joe was selling drugs in Albert's area, and he found out about it. So Joe came to me and asked if I could talk to Albert on his behalf, because he knew that I knew Albert. So I agreed to do him the favor.

"How'd it go with Albert?" Joe asks, as he leans in

across the rickety table inside the deli.

"Not a problem," I tell him. "Albert isn't going to mess with you anymore."

Joe leans back in the booth, letting out a huge breath as his shoulders go slack. "That's it?"

"Yeah," I say with a grin. "He asked me if I had anything to do with the selling, and when I told him no, he said I should take money off you." I let out a light chuckle. "I told him no. I wasn't going to do that, as long as I've known you, and now you're dating my sister." I shake my head.

Joe leans forward again, excitement in his voice. "Hey, why don't you be partners with me?" I look at him funny for a second, and he adds, "I'm serious. If it weren't for you, I'd still be having problems with Albert."

"All right," I say slowly, then nod. "Let's do it."

From this day forward, Joe and I are always together, day and night. We start moving around and selling coke.

I never left the deli job, for several reasons. One being it was a fun place to work, and it was where everybody hung out. I was friends with everyone there, and we'd all gather together and go to as many hockey, football, and baseball games as we could.

Working at the deli also became my home base, and besides the fact it was fun to be there, it was mainly for cover. I'd go there every day after school and started meeting more and more wiseguys and getting to know more street guys.

Of course the other dealers around had their own guys and their own connections, but because I was at the deli all the time, I became more and more convenient to them too, being able to help expand the business. I became really good friends with the man who owned the deli too. The deli owner, Joe O'Connor, never asked for a cut or tax. He was a real nice guy.

It's not like we really saved the money Joe and I made, which was hand over fist. We did really well for ourselves. We were all over the place, living in the fast lane and taking advantage of anything and everything we could for whatever it was worth. We'd just burn the money and live to the hilt. We went on vacations, we got close on a regular basis, and we started buying nice cars and all of the stuff I couldn't afford before. But I did put some money away, because I was getting ready to go to college—or so I thought.

Chapter 24

This isn't the first time I've been kicked out of the house, but this time it's for real. My father has had more than enough. I've taken things too far this time. He's done. Since coming back from Florida and having lost my baseball scholarship, I'm a lost cause.

I was a master at justifying all of my hustling schemes when my father would raise a questioning brow or argue about my misdemeanors, but selling drugs wasn't something I could prove to be reasonable. He was headstrong against them. Now, my father wants to ship me off to California, thinking this last-ditch effort of his will save me.

There's one thing my father has trouble digesting, though. He can't understand why I'm taking things to the extremes that I am, and he doesn't understand what's happening to me.

My father was a fighter—a street guy, but not a gangster. My dad was "fair," but the streets were not.

One could no longer afford to be fair on the streets. So in order to survive, I had to take things to a higher level, one my father would've never dreamed of.

He wasn't much of a witness to the things I was dealing with; he wasn't living on the same set of streets he grew up on decades ago.

Times have changed. The city has grown more sinister and dangerous with each passing day, which I didn't think was possible, but it's happening.

But my method of becoming extreme proves to be very dangerous, yet beneficial... for I'm already feared on the streets.

Before, when he'd throw me out, I'd go to a little club on 80th Street around the corner from the deli we all worked at. There was a couch in there, and when I'd get kicked out, I'd stay there for a night or two then just go home. So it never really lasted long. Sometimes I'd go to my aunt's house. I'd get kicked out for always being in trouble or fighting. I was somewhat of a good kid growing up, but now I just keep getting involved with dumb shit all the time. My dad saw it coming, understood the signs, because he's a street guy himself.

But through my high school years, I was getting more and more out of control. Chasing meaningless adrenaline rushes I'd become so addicted to. The other dumb shit was that I was hanging around the wrong people, like Albert Ruggiano, whose father is the boss, and he saw me being involved with Johnny Gebbert, who was selling drugs and cheating people from a young age.

Some of the 7N9 Gang members I'm hanging out with, because I'm staying with them every once in a while. And I'm playing hooky more and more and staying with Richard Langston.

Over the years, when he started seeing he was losing control of me, I started lying, saying I was going to work, he would beat me and try to chase me. He'd try to catch me; he'd try talking to me. But I was a lost cause by this point. It was too late.

~~*

The very second I walk in the door, my father greets me with a slap to the face. "Where have you been?" he yells in a rage. "I was worried!"

I take his slaps, just like I always do, with a stoic tolerance, not showing any emotion. He's more than pissed off. It's the first time I've stayed out until six in the morning, never coming home last night, and I didn't call or get a message to him.

"I thought you were dead somewhere in a ditch, just like everyone else!" He was past worried. He actually thought I'd become a victim like some of my friends.

"Why are you saying that?" He's never been worried like this before.

"Why?" he yells again, then lets loose a string of curse words in Albanian. He reaches behind his back and pulls out a bag of drugs from his back pocket then holds the bag up to my face, shaking it. "This is why! I was so on edge last night I couldn't sleep, so I went through your things and found these!"

"Is that all?" I ask, hoping he didn't see the rest.

For that answer, I get another slap to the side of the head, because he knows I'm trying to play him for a fool. "What are you doing with a gun and fifteen thousand dollars, Johnny?"

The screaming and fighting continues, and then he turns around, marching toward the bathroom, and I know what he's planning to do. I rush behind him all the way to the bathroom, but I can't stop him. I won't. I watch as he opens the baggy and empties every last ounce of coke into the toilet then proceeds to flush them.

"Dad," I say calmly, "I'm going to have problems with these buyers. That was actually worth a lot of money."

He turns to me, his eyes hard and his mouth tight, as he tells me between clenched teeth, "Well, that's your fucking problem. I don't give a shit. You're not selling them."

I scratch at my chin, wondering what the fuck I'm going to do now, but my father is already a step ahead of me.

"I'm sending you to California to live with your

uncle Sam," he callously informs me, an obvious last-ditch effort to try and redeem me. Uncle Sam is strict, but it's too late for anyone to save me.

"I'm not going to California," I tell him matter-of-factly.

He slaps me again, his voice full of heated anger. "The hell you aren't. You're going to live there, and you're going to get your shit straightened out."

I shake my head defiantly.

"Why, Johnny? Why you doing this?"

"Because I'm never going to be like you!" I roar. "Broke and desperate."

The second those words exit my mouth, I immediately regret them. I may as well have slapped him for the way he's looking at me right now. A brief moment of hurt flashes in his eyes then disappears. I'm upset with myself, so I turn around and head to my room, knowing I will regret saying those words to him for the rest of my life.

The house phone rings as I'm passing it. I hastily pick it up, barking out a gruff, "Yeah?"

It's one of my guys, and he sounds distressed.

"Calm down," I tell him. "Where are you?"

The second he tells me, I hang up the phone and head to my bedroom. My brother's in the room, and he looks up at me the second I enter.

"Johnny," he begins in a calm voice.

But I don't feel calm, so I snap at him, "What?"

"Don't you see yourself? You've turned into those

very guys you called crazy only a couple years ago."
He pauses, chewing on his bottom lip, wondering if
he should say anything else, because he knows I'm on
the edge of snapping.

"I see myself just fine," I bite back.

"No—no you're not." He tries to reason. "You've
turned completely fucking nuts. You can't even see
what you're becoming."

His words go ignored as I pull out my bottom
dresser drawer, grabbing some cash and another gun I
hid under some jeans. I wedge the gun between my
belt and jeans and get up to grab my jacket.

As I slip on my jacket, my brother asks, his voice
full of concern, "Where do you think you're going?"

Raising a brow, I glance his way, giving him a hard
look that says, *None of your business.* "Out." That's all I
tell him. I zip up my bomber jacket and leave the
house.

Stepping off the front porch, I hear my
grandfather calling out from behind, "Johnny—" His
voice cracking with worry. "—where you going?"

I ignore everyone as I jog the ten blocks or so to
the main strip, feeling the need all along to hurt
somebody.

The freezing winters we usually experience in
December is actually mild this year, and by the time
I've trekked the ten blocks or so to the main strip, I
almost feel like taking off my jacket. I head to one of
my local hangouts, and the first thing I see as I round

the corner is a handful of policemen handcuffing three of my friends.

The men in uniform glance my way and pause. I can see the look of recognition on their face as I come into view. I tilt my head to the side and look at them, giving them a sly grin. It's the type of grin that declares trouble is back and in full force. And right now, I'm untouchable. The very thought gives me a small rush of adrenaline.

I don't know why, but in this very moment, I feel so alive... so at home, even though I'm currently witnessing three of my buddies being handcuffed. I can't put into words what I'm feeling, but being back on the streets and in my own setting is giving me a true sense of belonging. Maybe it's because I've had the run of these streets since I was five, or the fact I'm familiar with so many people, all my childhood friends are here, and I know every facet of this city like the back of my hand. Yeah... this is home.

~~*

The one thing I do know, is I want to be the guy everybody wants to know yet fears, fears on a dangerous level. I'm living in a different world now, and by my late teens, I'm already caught up with money and power. I'm someone not to be messed with, and I'll be damned if I'm going to be the victim anymore.

It's as if I'm a racehorse and I'm full of adrenaline as I wait behind the closed gates, and then when they open, I'm one of the first to come out, full of fire and determination to be the one in the lead. And as each horse is giving it all they've got, I'm that horse in the rear that starts passing one horse after the other with a fierce resolve to win.

So I started to become that guy passing everybody one a time. I was making my move on everybody in the neighborhood, whether I was out hustling them, hurting them more than the next guy, getting a better product out on the street, or whatever it was—I was going to do it. I made that decision to move into that life, and I wasn't giving it up easily.

I learned how to watch people, to lay back and assess them. I was slick. I was able to be the one to take control and exploit their weaknesses. This was my best trait, I'd say, to be able to understand people and read them, and then manage them, pulling their cards if they wanted to match me with danger. I would step up the level and take bold chances, all to make them take a back seat to me and my aggression.

~~*

If you thought book 1 was an adventure…book 2 is a fast paced adrenaline rush. A"REAL LIFE" Thriller of one suspenseful event overlapping another.

TO PURCHASE THE NEXT BOOK IN SERIES

VISIT MY WEBSITE
www.JohnAliteDarkestHour.com

~~*

Find out what happened during John Alite's college days!!
Get deleted Scenes and Chapters for FREE &
keep up with news events PLUS,
be the first to get sneak peaks of Darkest Hour

Book 2 before anyone else!
VISIT MY WEBSITE ◈ ➜
www.JohnAliteDarkestHour.com

BookBub has a New Release Alert.
Not only can you check out the latest deals, but you can get also an email
when I release my next book by following me here
◈ ➜ www.bookbub.com/authors/s-c-pike

Photographs

Matthew, Fatima, Ali, & Fred Alite John
Alite's father, grandparents, & uncle

(Left) John Alite (right) Brother, Jimmy Alite

John Alite & his great aunt Alba
(His grandpa's Sister who lived upstairs
who was like another
grandmother figure to John.)

John & Jimmy Alite with their uncle Dan and
uncle Fred (Matthew Alite's brother)
Woodhaven home

John, Jimmy, Matthew Alite, &
Brothers Kevin and Tim Jones
(Kevin's hat is backward)

JimmyAlite growing up in
Woodhaven home

1976 Rich-Haven baseball team.
Uncle Fred (far right)
John Alite (front, 2nd from right)
Mr. Brian Jones (far left)

John Alite & Father, Matthew Alite

John Alite
High school Prom before picking picking up his
date Terri

Want to see more pictures
Get news updates and more
Visit my website:
www..JohnAliteDarkestHour.com

Author Notes

How is it that John Alite could move back to the very area where he killed for a living, shot and maimed countless enemies, having left a ton of wreckage and chaos behind?

The question we must all ask ourselves on so many different levels is — WHY?

Why doesn't any former boss from any crime family, Captain of any crew, or any soldier who worked the streets, not live like John Alite? Why do all those so called killers, who were "made men", stay hidden away in other states while existing under different identities?

Why did John Alite turn down the government witness protection program? What does John Alite have that so many other's don't?

Besides the nonsensical, ignorant critics who only know how to write obscenities on social media, cowering behind their keyboards like a insolent five year old while hiding behind their mother's skirts — why isn't the mafia making an attack on his life? John Alite is very much public, living on his terms which basically challenges anyone who was ever after him to step out and approach him to a duel.

This is John's question to everyone — *WHY?*

~~*

Through a life of heartache, betrayal, and loss, comes a story of grace, healing, and redemption. But somethings never truly change, do they? The very fabric of John's being is comprised of a sober fearlessness with a propensity to dole out violence the very moment he suspects a threat without a second's hesitation.

This amazing man didn't hesitate to open up his heart and soul to me. He's allowed me to capture his life's story in a way that goes far beyond just the facts of the mob life. And as the months have passed between us, I've come to understand John in a new light. I've been able to tap into his complex mind and extract not only his very thoughts, but his reasonings, and thought processes. John keeps his emotions under lock and key, but I was determined to open those doors too.

John's story goes beyond unique, I believe it's different than anything anyone has ever written before. It's simply not in me to write a story without being able to pull the reader in… making them feel as if they're walking in the main character's shoes themselves. I wanted the reader to feel the anger, the laughter, the tears, and heartache of loss while experiencing the blood pumping adrenaline that John lived out on a day to day basis.

~~*

I've never been one to conform to traditions, and I adhere to very few social protocols and procedures. I don't disrespect authority, but I suppose I'm still considered a rebel of sorts. My father raised me to be independent, strong-minded, and to question everything. I've always taken the initiative to investigate all things for myself in order to formulate my very own conclusions, taking no one's word as gospel. I have an unquenchable thirst for knowledge, new challenges, and uncovering untapped territories, and when I want something I go after it with a vengeance.

I was writing under my pen name when I began to investigate the world of the New York mafia for a new book I was writing. Of course, reading a few books on this subject simply wouldn't do. I've always had this inane desire to master subjects and topics to the absolute extreme. So I began to devour dozens and dozens of books, left and right, one after the other. I was reading true story undercover biographies, and more mafia and true crime stories than what should've been considered normal. For five straight months, I was digesting close to four books a week, soaking in all the information I could find on the mafia.

But the very moment I stumbled upon George Anastasia's book, Gotti's Rules... everything around me came to a screeching halt. I had found myself overly engrossed, and beyond intrigued by John Alite's story. I never read books for a second time, never, but I was in awe of Mr. Anastasia's talent and his ability to write John's story.

I had to contact him.
I had more questions.
I wanted answers.

George Anastasia had articulated the facts so intriguingly well, I didn't walk away from this book having mafia questions... Instead, I had soul searching ones. I had an uncontrollable and overwhelming need to know what made this man tick... what made John Alite... be John Alite. I had to know how he survived the series of events that played out in his life, and what made him want to turn his life around, and what was his breaking point. I started out with every intention of writing John's life story as one novel, but with careful peeling away of all the complex layers from his history, he revealed more layers within layers that lead to more questions, and I had to keep backing up his timeline. I've described John as trying to assemble a five-thousand piece puzzle while being blindfolded. This is when I knew one book wasn't enough to tell his story.

John lived a series of events that didn't happen simply one after the other... everything overlapped and intertwined, becoming matrix of chaos... There are too many elaborate circumstances from his childhood on that have come together to form this complex and highly intelligent man.

When I met John for the first time, I was struck by the unspoken, powerful presence he exuded the moment he walked into the lobby. Besides him being a brick wall of pure muscle, charisma and self-confidence radiated off him in droves, yet at the same time he displayed a genuine humbleness.

I must have some fear-factor meter missing from my genetics, because I didn't feel any intimidation or nervousness upon meeting

John Alite for the first time. My husband always told me there's a fine line between bravery and stupidity... I'd like to think I'm neither. I'm just me which includes a decent dose of the unconventional. My gut never steers me wrong, and I had a gut feeling that John truly had changed for the better. He has a story to tell, and a strong desire to help young kids and inspire them to stay off the streets.

Those closest to me, who have expressed their concern for my safety, because of the sensitive subject matter I'm writing about, my immediate response to them was:

"I've always put my faith in God, asking for his guidance and his protection. He has blessed me with awesome guardian angels! Yes... I may work them overtime... but they knew that when they took on the job!"

Within the first hour of meeting John I did, however, need a drink in order to let my true self out of it's cage, but this had zero to do with the fact I was getting ready to interview a notorious criminal. One who served a vast amount of prison time for serious crimes he committed. Understand firstly, I have a constant struggle with being an introvert... and despite my quirky, unfiltered, yet fun-loving personality, my jobs require me to act as if I'm not. I put on my game face everyday, playing the highly interactive professional business woman while running two separate businesses. So until I get to know someone, I sometimes need an icebreaker to relax so people can see behind my exterior walls and get to know the real me.

I had also spent significant time with John's immediate family so I could get a better feel for his early childhood and how the family's dynamics operate. In one particular circumstance, I witnessed first hand, the temper he battles to control on a consistent basis. It all started with a phone call... and then his emotions slowly unraveled over the next thirty minutes. I could feel his struggle as he tried valiantly to maintain his composure. Heated anger began to boil up from the depths of his soul, and there was no stopping it. He was like a ticking time bomb, a volcano about to erupt. With morbid curiosity, I had to sit back and watch this event unfold. I didn't give a second thought to John's past and what violence would rain down on the recipient of his anger. I couldn't stop myself from watching with rapt fascination how everything within him finally exploded. It was like watching fireworks on the fourth of July, his vocals being the first thing to go off.

My God — that deep, raspy voice of his — it projected outward like a thunderous roar, or an untamed lion staking his claim over the lands. This outburst should've been scary to me, but I was more mesmerized than anything. I'm certain anyone within a hundred feet of his voice was turning around and walking the other way... quickly, I might add. I remained quiet, staying out of the way all the while taking mental notes, and giving him the space he needed to work through his personal storm.

Later that evening as we continued our interviewing, we broached the subject of his temper. John said matter-of-factly, "That explosion of anger was nothing... you should see me when I'm really angry."

I found myself damn near bursting out with laughter at that statement. The missing common sense gene I didn't own was screaming at me from some far away distance, "Abort... abort this project. Run — woman — run."

I've also seen John's moods shift in the blink of an eye, going from a relaxed, smiling, jovial state — to the cold, hard, bone chilling tough-guy persona he keeps hidden in the dark recesses of his soul. This quick change in behavior did give me pause... but only for a brief moment, because I know that tough-guy would never be unleashed on me. I already have a deep level of understanding of him, how he thinks, and how he operates. I have the utmost confidence, respect, and trust in him, and above all, I can see the good in his soul.

But this right here... John's compassion, kindness, charity, and lionhearted spirit... this is what I want the world to see... who I want the world to know... I want people to understand the real John Alite. This highly caring and giving man who'd give his last dollar to help someone in need, who simply had the cards stacked against him since birth. He was living the only way he knew how while growing up in the most turbulent and violent times in New York's history...

He was on the street — and the goal was to survive.

Made in the USA
Middletown, DE
20 April 2019